JESUS SAID

A NEW LOOK AT THE GOSPELS

By Mary Saurer-Smith

Copyright © 2024 Mary Saurer-Smith All rights reserved

No part of this book may be reproduced, or stored in a retrieval system, or transmitted in any form or by any means, electronic, mechanical, photocopying, recording, or otherwise, without express written permission of the publisher.

ISBN: 9798877463585

Imprint: Independently published

CONTENTS

Chapter One

. Recorded History of the Jews

Chapter Two

. Books about Jesus by people who knew him.

Chapter Three

. What Jesus Taught according to Matthew

Chapter Four

. Jesus As a Ransom

Chapter Five

. The Great Pre-Planned Drama Begins

Chapter Six

. Gospel Writers Differ About the End

Chapter Seven

. Excerpts From the Book of John

Chapter Eight

. The Jesus Followers

Chapter Nine

. A Militant Form of Christianity Arises

Preface

This book is for people who like to think or study independently.

It can be a provocative study guide for anyone who would like to facilitate a discussion group using this material, whether in agreement with the material or not. The reader or group member is encouraged to consider these concepts with an open mind and then contemplate them in private.

My objective is to promote the message of the Master, Jesus, and to stimulate your curiosity. My hope is that you will be enticed to read his message again and draw conclusions for yourself. If this study guide stirs up questions in your mind, then it has served its purpose. If it gives you answers that can accelerate you on your spiritual journey, then it has more than served its purpose.

Many thanks to my son, Kenny Hines, and my good friend Steven Michael Hall, a photographer and former journalist from Tulsa, OK, for the many hours they spent editing this book.

Chapter ONE
Recorded History of the Jews

Knowing the history of the Jews is crucial to understanding the audience to which Jesus' spoke. Their story:

Desiring to form a monarchy as other nationalities had done, rather than just be a band of people with no way to collect commonwealth, the ancient Israelites demanded that a king be appointed for them to help them prosper in the world. Until that point, the Israelite states, established by Jacob's 12 sons and their descendants after Moses had rescued them from Egypt, had been ruled for centuries by judges who used the ancient scriptures of Moses for their rulings. Reluctantly, the judges bent to popular demand and appointed Saul as first king of the Israelite monarchy.

King David, second king of the Israelites, whose home was in the area known as *Jerusalem,* built a palace there. He took possession of the ancient Holy Books, which held the teachings of Moses and other books about their history, and had a new tabernacle built to house the books. King David proclaimed Jerusalem as the capital and the official center of worship for all Israelite tribes. David's son, Solomon, inherited the throne and was considered the wisest of all Israelite kings. He collected enormous wealth for the office of the royalty and expanded the wealth of Israel as a nation.

The tribe of Benjamin had been excommunicated from the House of Israel long before David's time, so actually they were down to 11 tribes of Israel as a nation.

Because of disagreement over religious issues, many of the other tribes seceded from subservience to the House of David (they denied the lineage of David as the line of the kings).

This diminished the importance of Jerusalem for a time because only two tribes stayed connected to the House of David and lived in Jerusalem. The other 10 Israeli tribes had settled in cities near Jerusalem but did not communicate with the Jerusalem inhabitants.

Several hundred years of war followed, in which efforts were made by various countries to capture Jerusalem and areas surrounding it. These wars culminated in material and social progress for Jerusalem, followed by 100 years of the greatest prosperity the Israelites had ever known.

Sixty-three years before the birth of Jesus, the powerful and expanding Roman Empire conquered and claimed the city of Jerusalem (just as the Israelites had captured it from the Babylonians about 1,500 years before). The Roman Empire encompassed almost all of the civilized world and was considered the dominating power of the world.

During their reign, the Romans permitted the citizens of Jerusalem, Jews as they called them, to continue inhabiting Jerusalem as their Holy City and to retain their laws and customs for ruling their people. They were not slaves. The only stipulation was that Roman law would supersede the Jewish laws in case of a conflict and that the Jews would pay taxes to the Roman government (just as the people of our individual states pay taxes to the nation as well as to the state).

The Jews concept of the end of the world is related to the end of the Roman Empire and restoration of their reign in Jerusalem.

In a close look at the difference between what the Gospel writers reported and what they believed we see that, when there was a discrepancy between Jesus' teaching and the ancient books, the Gospel writers held Moses and his books as superior to the words of Jesus even though they claimed Jesus as their Messiah.

The truth of what Jesus really taught, compared to common beliefs of what he taught, is in the Gospels for individual seekers to find, but his followers could not release identifying with the teachings of Moses, their foundation premise. Moses wrote the first four books of the Old Testament of the Christian Bible. The beliefs in Moses' teachings were carried over into Christianity by Paul and other Israelis who were founding leaders of the Christian movement.

When we set aside all pre-conceived ideas of God and the teachings of Moses, we can watch and hear Jesus without reference to any religion, or the story of Adam and Eve with its' explanation of why people experience troubles in this world. Jesus said, "In this world is tribulation" and he gave a different reason about why that is so. By releasing the basic premise of the people that he came to teach, we can clearly see Jesus' message of what is and always has been true about the nature of God. We can accept the gift of our opportunity to establish and maintain an individual relationship with God. Jesus tells us how to do that.

CHAPTER TWO

Books About Jesus by People Who Knew Him

There are only nine well known books available to the world that were written about Jesus by people who actually knew him when he was in the world.

Of those nine books by those who knew him, only two are written as *biographical accounts* with quotes of what he said and descriptions of what he did. The writers of those two books were the disciples Matthew and John, who lived, traveled, and worked with Jesus during his three-year ministry.

Two other biographical accounts, Mark and Luke, were written by men who did not know him. They wrote as students of his disciples. Mark and Luke wrote about Jesus' life but did not know him personally and were not a part of his ministry before the crucifixion.

The books of Matthew, John, Luke, and Mark are called "The Gospels".

Concerning the other seven books written by people who actually knew him; two are by Jesus' brothers, James, and Jude; two are by the disciple Peter, and three are by the disciple John. As inspiring as they are, these books are all letters or sermons delivering the author's concept of Jesus ministry. They tie the books of the Old Testament together with the writer's concept of Jesus' identity and mission. When they reported a difference, these writers gave greater authority to the Israelite's history and books than to Jesus' words. They attempted to spread his message as they understood it without defying their heritage. This examination of what Jesus actually said will be focused largely upon the biographical accounts of the two writers who knew Jesus, traveled with him, and were his direct students and assistants.

Paul, whose books make up much of the New Testament, never met Jesus and did not write a biographical book about him. He wrote about his personal conversion experience with the spirit of Jesus and his beliefs as a result of that experience.

As we examine the books, we will see that Jesus named his identity and his purpose for coming into the world. He spoke often of every person's potential to learn about the nature and truth of God directly through the Holy Spirit, and how to do that. Jesus taught that the nature of God is not as those ancient scriptures describe him. He presented a quite different description of the Creator. Fortunately for us, even though these writers clung to the old concepts of God, as given by Moses, they reported the Messiah's words that agreed with their beliefs as well as those that did not.

Moses, author of the first few books of the Israelis' Holy Books, had given his explanation of why there is pain and difficulty in this world. He said that God had punished the entire race of humanity because the original inhabitants of earth had disobeyed Him. The punishment would last through all generations until God decided to forgive. For centuries they tried to obey the rules set out by Moses in hopes that God would release the condemnation and set their race free from the human condition of sorrows. Their Prophets had predicted that God would someday send a Savior to teach them more about how to please the Creator, and to lift the curse that Moses had told them about.

They were afraid to release the old teachings of Moses with his explanation of why humanity experiences pain and perils, lest more perils come upon them. Before Moses the only concept of God that these descendants of Abraham and Isaac held was that he spoke to them in dreams to guide them in what they were to do. The founders of the Jewish religion worshipped the books of Moses as absolute truth. Jesus said that the true nature of God is not vengeful and punishing as Moses had taught, but merciful and forgiving.

Psychics, called prophets, predicted that a teacher would be sent by God to teach them how to gain their freedom from the curse. If they did not accept him, the punishment of their race would remain in effect until they accepted his gift. They did not perceive themselves as individuals but as parts of a group and they all were required to believe the same thing in order to be saved from the curse. One who did not hold the accepted beliefs and obey the rules set out by Moses was believed to keep the curse going. That one became an outcast with punishment or shunning from the leaders.

Understanding what the Israelis believed and how their history led them to hold such a concept of God, Jesus explained that they could each establish a personal relationship with God. He appealed to them to let God be their individual guide to spiritual freedom and explained how to establish a personal relationship with their Creator.

Jesus invited them to release old beliefs about God and their worship of Moses' view of how life began on earth. The Master challenged them to accept new ideas that would set them free from fear of defying the religion and its leaders.

Introduction to The Gospel Writers

Matthew wrote as a historian to convince the Jewish people that Jesus of Nazareth had been, and was, the Messiah (teacher) whose entry had been predicted by Jewish prophets for thousands of years. Because of this way of looking at it, Matthew's focus was on genealogy, prophecies of the Jewish Holy Books, Jesus' knowledge of those ancient scriptures, and the Jewish teachings of resurrection.

He emphasized the importance of accepting that Jesus was sent by God to save the Jewish people. Matthew said that those who did not accept this gift would not have God's forgiveness for the original sin of Adam and Eve. That sin was, according to Moses, God's curse, and the cause of all human suffering. He perceived God as a tyrannical and vengeful dictator who could show mercy and love if He were strictly obeyed and worshipped. Because of Matthew's belief in the ancient Jewish scriptures, he could not see the contradictions between the messages of the Jews and the words of Jesus.

After the resurrection, Matthew also emphasized the predictions that Jesus had made of his resurrection after death, saying this was proof that Jesus was the Messiah they had expected (even though he denied many of Jesus' words and held Moses' teachings as a higher truth than what Jesus said.) The stories and rules of Moses were Mathew's basic premise for reasoning. Even so, Matthew was an excellent reporter of those things he witnessed and selected to emphasize. It is unfortunate that he did not examine more closely the words of Jesus, accept them as Truth and release his old beliefs as Jesus taught. The Old Testament of the Christian Bible is carried over from those ancient beliefs and history of the Israelites.

John wrote as a philosopher. He wrote to convince anyone who would read his material that Jesus was God, who had become frustrated with assigning mere men to give his message to one another and decided to come in person. (If Jesus is God, why would Jesus say that the Holy Spirit can give more knowledge than he because that knowledge is directly from God)?

John wrote from *his* belief that God had come down to earth in person to deliver his message to the Jews, because Jews were the lawmakers for the Israelites. Due to his belief, that Jesus is God, John's emphasis was on the miracles that Jesus performed. John never considered relating these miracles to the idea that the healed person accepted that illness was not a punishment from God. Jesus often said that a change in belief had done the healing.

Changing the mind is the principle by which psychic activity, hypnotism, or masterful knowledge of the universal laws can influence healing in a person. In the writer's mind, only God or Satan could do such magical things, and Jesus was clearly not Satan. The miracle healings, the telepathic awareness, and the predictions that Jesus made were all used to support John's theory that this was God. John also emphasized the fact that Jesus predicted his own crucifixion and that it happened just as he said it would. (In contradiction, John reports that he, himself, was rather surprised when Jesus was resurrected, and that Jesus had not told them this would happen!)

John's major theme is sacrifice, because he believed that God had made a sacrifice in order to free the Jews from punishment for the "original sin". Interestingly enough Jesus said, "I will have mercy, *not* sacrifice."

Regardless of John's contrary beliefs, many of the words and actions of Jesus during his three-year ministry were recorded by John. John reported what Jesus said about his own identity and mission, what he taught about God, and what he said about the Kingdom of God. Even though he reported correctly, as he tried to understand, he denied what did not fit the old story of God according to Moses.

Mark and Luke, the other two Gospel writers, were like journalists who collected stories and writings and interviewed people who knew Jesus. There were no copyright laws then, so they were free to consolidate the writings and the stories into books of their own. Notice how Luke begins his book.

These two writers wrote their books to emphasize their beliefs (as is commonly done among writers). Both of these writers were **followers of Paul** who never knew Jesus when he was in this world. He took on a mission to write and teach years after the crucifixion. Their emphasis was on *supporting Paul's concept of Jesus' identity and mission.*

Paul, author of many of the New Testament books, was a dedicated and charismatic militant in the Jewish government at the time of the personal conversion experience that he reported. He did not know Jesus before the crucifixion, nor did he witness Jesus' ministry. He did not claim to give up any of the treasured Jewish beliefs for which he had fought so hard in his former persecution of Jesus' followers. He simply expanded his belief in the Jewish scriptures to concur that Jesus was the expected Messiah and that life after death is a reality. This set the foundation for Christianity as opposed to Judaism which did not believe in an afterlife. He taught that now every human being was free from God's punishment for the original sin only if they would concur that Jesus' was a sacrifice or scapegoat for all humanity to save only those who admitted that he was the expected Messiah. Paul's focus, and that of his followers, was on salvation or exemption from punishment.

When Paul first reported his own experience to the apostles that Jesus had appointed, they were skeptical. Jesus had come to meet with them, give them assignments, and coach them several times after his crucifixion and resurrection. He had called them friends instead of servants, saying that friends know what their leader's plans are and servants do not. Because of this, they insisted he would have told them if he had appointed another apostle. Jesus had assigned each of them a specific territory to cover in the spreading of his message. Paul announced that he would be covering all territories and that he was not limited to a specific territory. This meant he would be working in the same areas that they had been specifically assigned by Jesus and giving a different view. Luke was Paul's right-hand-man in helping to broadcast Paul's message.

Jesus' message that God does not punish and his message of freedom to pursue God directly, without fear, was all but buried under the new yoke of religious rules that Paul imposed upon his followers. Paul promoted the same fear-based message that he had always supported and created even more rules to follow.

Mark, a follower of Paul and friend of Peter, formed much of his book from interviews with the original disciples, and a great deal of his work is very similar in content to that of the book of Matthew. He was a close friend of the disciple Peter before Peter and Paul had a major conflict (do you wonder what that was about?) and went their separate ways. Mark then made his choice to serve under Paul's ministry and to support Paul's interpretation completely. His writings reflect many of Paul's conclusions.

Luke, follower of Paul, was a physician and an attorney who was in awe of the miraculous healings that Jesus was reported to have done. He was also a dedicated convert of Paul. Paul's goal was to use the advent of Jesus' crucifixion to promote him as a sacrificial lamb (scapegoat) who was slain for the original sin and all subsequent sins—past, present, and future—as God's gift to those who would accept Jesus as God.

Jesus' Message Compared to Common Beliefs

As we begin our study of *Jesus'* message, let us keep in mind that the belief system just described is the belief system of the people he must attempt to inform, influence, and teach in an effort to have them release their old beliefs about the nature of God based on the stories given by Moses.

He began his "Sermon on The Mount" by confirming ideas that are true and explaining new concepts. His mission was to lift as many as he could out of their burdensome, oppressing, and enslaving belief system into the freedom to seek and find direct communion with God and freedom to live as directed in prayer. His message was intended to encourage them to break free from a tribal or religious relationship to God and to embrace the concept of a personal and individual relationship with God.

Due to their belief that this world would eventually become "heaven", his listeners were fearful of consequences. In their effort to understand, they always went back to social concerns, responsibilities, worldly concerns, and human relations when questioning him. Jesus did not discount the considerations of right human relations. He merely put them in their proper perspective as secondary to a personal relationship with God. He gave many parables and stories as examples of what he considered right human relations, with an emphasis on empathetic treatment of one another. He tried to assure them that he had not come to speak against their social interaction laws given by Moses, and he even consolidated those ten laws into one objective. That suggested objective and formula for right human relations was to simply "do to others what you would want them to do to you."

Jesus said the teaching of morality, ethics, social law, and accountability to one another for social cooperation had already been given by Moses. He explained that he, himself, had come to correct their beliefs about the nature of God and heaven. He said his mission was to tell them what *Heaven* really is and how they could experience it via an individual relationship with God through the Holy Spirit.

Some perceived his message; others did not. Some focused on his human relations message and missed his explanation of Heaven completely. Some focused on his healings of the sick and the other miracles he did, saying he was not sent from God as he said, but that he was God. Some said that God gave him these powers to do the miracles so that he could convince the people to believe in him. Others said that Satan gave him these powers to do the miracles so he could fool the people into believing. Some said that he was teaching something different than what they believed and called him a charlatan; for if he truly were representing God, he would be supporting what they believed and would be preparing them for battle. They did not know that the battle against their oppressor was to be the internal battle against this belief system that oppressed them by portraying God as a vengeful tyrant.

CHAPTER THREE
What Jesus Taught According to Matthew

Sermon on the Mount

As recorded in three of the four Gospels.

Key ideas to note:
Using a Bible to read the suggested passages will add tremendously to the readers understanding. (Any version of the Bible will serve the same purpose)

Much of the Sermon is made up of direct quotes from ancient Jewish Scripture. Jesus examines and comments on those existing beliefs. He speaks of actions as causes, and certain results as their natural effects, either immediate or in the future rather than punishments from God. Jesus never suggests that God will offer any punishment or reward for doing or not doing what is addressed. In overview, the Sermon on the Mount is a lesson on the natural effect of action as it relates to the human condition.

Matthew 5:3

This is a reference to the books of Isaiah, Proverbs, and Psalms. It is a very common belief of the Jews that kept them from losing faith in the heaven to come while they suffered from poverty in this world.

Matthew 5:4

Refers to the book of Isaiah, chapter 61:2-3. It is another common belief that helped them to overcome the grief from the frequent losses they encountered. He said that emotional recovery was an assurance they could count on receiving over and over again.

Matthew 5:5
Refers to the book of Numbers 12:3. This group often waged war and believed defeat to be God's continued punishment, with the punishment of keeping them subservient slaves. They clung to the hope of someday inheriting the earth for their entire tribe while God would "punish" their offenders.

Matthew 5:6
Refers to a prophesy that if this tribe of people would but seek to know righteousness, they would be filled with it.

Matthew 5:7
Refers to Psalms 41:1 in which David sang that those who expressed mercy would receive mercy from God, and their emotional pain would be decreased.

Matthew 5:8
Refers to Psalms 15:1. It explains why the prophets and some kings were able to see and hear God while others were not. Purity of heart (harmless feelings and motives) made the difference.

Matthew 5:9
Jesus now begins his own "blessed are" statements. He knew of the persecutions that his followers would have to endure both from the stoic Jews and from the Romans after he was gone. This idea would certainly have encouraged them if only they would accept that God was not behind the reviling, the persecutions, the lies, and their outcast from the Jews. He said that people were responsible for those conditions, and in the face of eternity, it was just a passing thing.

Key points made by Jesus in the Sermon

Matthew 5:18
He states that both the Earth and heaven are temporary domiciles and that the law (of cause and effect) will remain in effect as long as the universe endures. (Until both heaven and Earth pass away.)

Matthew 7:12
Jesus defines precisely what he means when he says, "the law" (using the book of Leviticus as backup for his claim).

Matthew 6:32
He implores his listeners to stop believing that to work for their survival and the survival of their family is the spiritual purpose for living. He said even the Gentiles practice that. He said that the individual's *spiritual work is to seek the Kingdom of God and God's righteousness.*

Matthew 5:20 through Matthew 7:12
The Master reveals what true righteousness is. He says that their law has spoken only of behaviors, but *the feelings and thoughts that one has inside the mind are equally important.* He says if one is doing something in thought and feeling, that action is also being done in spirit. He says that the way to develop righteousness is to become an expression of righteous *thinking.* He does not say that God will punish anyone who does not become righteous in their thinking. He says that the *progress toward realization of heaven (full awareness of God) will be delayed if righteousness is not practiced.*

Matthew 5:27 through Matthew 5:48
Jesus insists that people are capable of deciding what they will think, desire, and feel, and that persons have the power of will and choice for shaping their own attitudes. (Their belief was that Satan or God, or some other person made them feel and think as

they did. *Also, they believed it did not matter what was in the mind. Their entire focus was on outer behavior and speech.)*

With this astounding announcement, Jesus continues to say what some of the righteous attitudes, feelings and thoughts toward others would be—a willingness to cooperate with those in power over you, a feeling of agape love toward all people no matter their behavior toward you or others, and forgiveness (non-vengeance/non-punishment) as the key to this kind of love. He said this is the way that God loves.

The advice he gave was in relation to the trend of the times and the political atmosphere in which the Jews lived. The Roman law was that the Romans could ask any Jewish person to give him his coat or to loan him something or to carry his load for him, and the Jewish person was required by civil law to do whatever he was asked to do.

The Jews commonly rebelled and were thrown into prison or beaten severely. They were free to make their religious laws but were not in any position to make civil laws. Jesus' advice was to look upon such demands as an opportunity to cooperate with the governing laws. This way they would be demonstrating a growth in righteousness as well as avoiding society's punishment for their rebellion.

Matthew 5:19
Jesus suggests there are different degrees of righteousness in the kingdom of heaven where souls with various qualities of spiritual advancement will reside, rather than that all will be of equal degrees of righteousness and understanding.

Matthew 6:33 and Matthew 7:13
He emphasizes the importance of practicing the way or the path that one will take to advance toward developing righteousness

and seeking the Kingdom of Heaven. He speaks of the importance of ignoring that which distracts from one's purpose as a personal relationship with God is growing.

Matthew 6:1 and 7:22
Jesus emphasizes the importance of integrity. He warns that following the lead of those who say one thing and do, say or think the opposite is certainly to follow the blind man. He advises to follow only those who do as they teach. This means they are sincere and are not motivated by the hunger for money, glory, honor, self-righteousness, superiority, or power. He suggests that to give much attention to one who is not on your path is delaying yourself, instead of advancing toward greater heights through your own inner sense of heaven.

Jesus quotes from the book of Numbers that one of the recorded messages from God was that He would have no communion with those who have merely given psychic prophecies and have worked miracles as their only spiritual demonstration. He says the approach to your Kingdom of God is not advanced by such things.

Matthew 7:24
Jesus says that those who hear and believe and follow through with the things that he teaches are wise people. Regardless of what comes their way, they will hold to what he taught plus righteous behaviors; thus maintaining the momentum of a spiritual direction.

Matthew 6:5-8
Jesus advises not to pray for the purpose of impressing other people with one's relationship to God.

Matthew 6:9 through 6:13
Jesus suggests a pattern for prayer that begins with acknowledgment of one's relationship to God, reverence toward God's

name, a request to experience the Kingdom of God, acknowledgment that God's will is done in heaven, and request that God's will be done on earth.

The second phase of Jesus' suggested pattern for prayer is to ask for two things. First to ask that the basic needs be filled this day. Next to ask for forgiveness in case one has knowingly or unknowingly done that which was painful or harmful to another whether physical or emotional.

". . . forgive us our trespasses as we forgive those who trespass against us;" (knowingly or unknowingly).

The next phase is a request for guidance into activities, relationships and opportunities that do not cause deviation from the spiritual focus and will help maintain activities and relationships that serve the intent of Spiritual Righteousness. (Avoiding such distractions makes self-discipline and right choices easier.)

Amen (And so it is.)

Matthew 6:14-15

Jesus explains the forgiveness clause, warning people to give to others the forgiveness they themselves want from God, and that their own willingness to set others free from punishment determines the degree to which they will be set free from the agony of vengeance. He did not say that God would punish if one does not forgive. He said that one's own sense of being free from condemnation is a cause-and-effect result of not holding grudges in one's mind. An attitude of needing others to pay or suffer "consequences" is cause of much emotional pain.

After the Sermon on the Mount

When Jesus had concluded this Sermon, the people were shocked because he taught as if he knew God personally and not as one who had read a message somewhere. Matthew says that multitudes of people followed him when he came down from the mountain and as he walked, he encountered lepers and healed them with a touch, demonstrating spontaneous compassion (mercy) without going out of his way to find people to heal. Then he taught that when one believes that God does not ever will them to be ill, they will give themselves permission to accept healing *if and when it is available to them*. He attempted many times to point out the difference between the cause-and-effect activity/results of the Universe and the will of the Creator.

The word of his ability to heal physical illnesses spread rapidly (result of convincing them that God does not will their illness). His followers came from everywhere and would not let him have any privacy.

Jesus again stressed that the feelings and thoughts held in one's mind are of primary importance, and he named *faith in God's benevolence as the key to allowing healing to take place.* Historically these people had believed that illness was a punishment from God. *They believed that to accept illness without effort to change it was divine.* To see a man undo what God had done seemed confusing to them, so rather than admit they were wrong, they decided God was changing His mind in order to show them His power through this man.

Matthew 8:1-22

Matthew describes a scene in which Jesus has accepted the request for many healings. Still a huge crowd is gathered waiting for more healings and miracles from him. We will find Jesus many times demonstrating a decisive and assertive personality by deciding when he will and when he will not serve the crowds. He does not sacrifice his will at all but exercises it boldly throughout his ministry.

- Jesus said to his disciples, "Let us go to the other side," and he left the crowd which was seeking his healing and attention without offering them what they were demanding.

- A scribe (writer) wanted to go with him wherever he might go. Jesus warned that this ministry would require him to travel with no comforts of home, sleeping wherever he might be.

- Jesus gave his first comment on social and family responsibility as compared to submission to following the urge of the Holy Spirit to enter into a spiritual way of life and ignore everything that would lead one's consciousness into different interests. His example was made with a disciple who had reservations about suddenly changing his lifestyle. He had social, family, and worldly responsibilities that would delay him from following the Christ. The disciple asked permission of Jesus saying, "Let me go first and bury my father."

  Jesus' response was clear to some, confusing to others: "Follow me, and let the dead bury their dead."

Jesus demonstrates the creative power of mind for things other than physical healing.

Matthew 8:26

Jesus stopped a storm on the sea as he traveled by boat. When the boat landed, he encountered two men who were possessed by evil entities from the lower dimensions (or possessed by devils). He communicated with them and, knowing that he was about to perform an exorcism, these evil entities begged not to be sent out of the physical form altogether but instead to be sent into the pigs nearby. He accommodated their request; but the pigs went wild because of the blind emotional fear that resulted, and they committed suicide. Then the whole city came out and asked him to leave because they did not trust anyone with so much strange power. He accommodated them and went back home.

The Power of Forgiveness
Matthew 9:1

In this next phase of his teaching ministry, Jesus introduces forgiveness again, another great power of the mind that these people seem to know little about.

The Hebrews fully believed that when someone was ill, it was a punishment from God for sins committed. Ignoring their belief, Jesus merely acted on his own belief. He said to a weak and crippled man, "Son, be of good cheer; your sins are forgiven you." (a demonstration of mercy)

But some of the reporters in the crowd were shocked and believed that he was saying he had more power than God and could challenge God by undoing punishment that God had given because of unforgiven sins.

Jesus knew their thoughts and tried to reason with them. "Which do you think is harder to do, to tell a crippled man to walk or to say your sins are forgiven you? But just to show you that people have power on earth to forgive sins, watch this."

Turning to the sick man he commanded, "Arise, take up your bed, and go to your house."

Relieved of his false belief, the man did as he was told.

This crowd then glorified God for giving such power to men as to forgive sins. It was a whole new concept to them.

Matthew becomes a personal disciple of Jesus.
Matthew 9:9-11

After that demonstration of the power to forgive, Matthew reports that Jesus saw him at work and invited him, saying, "Follow me." Matthew followed, and they went with his other disciples to a restaurant where publicans and sinners sat down with him and his disciples to eat.

The "sinners" were people who had been excommunicated from the Jewish community, and the custom was to have no communication or involvement with those who were outcast. They were considered to be uncooperative sinners. (dead to the Jewish community).

Pharisees were present, and they challenged Jesus' wisdom in allowing such people to eat with him.

Jesus not needed by everyone.
Matthew 9:12-13

Jesus explained that some people already have developed and are expressing spiritual righteousness. They habitually experience righteous thoughts and feelings and do not need a teacher of righteousness. *I have not come to ask the righteous to change but to ask the sinners to change. A well person needs no doctor, but the sick do. Try to learn what I meant when I said, "I will have mercy, not sacrifice."*

(Sacrifice was one of the key points of the Jewish religion, and now Jesus was saying that sacrifice is not necessary, but mercy/compassion is.)

More healings and more exorcisms took place as Jesus' fame grew. Thousands came to see him and hear his message. Once he had gained great fame, Jesus returned to teaching in the synagogues instead of on hilltops. He was a Jewish priest/rabbi.

Matthew 9:35-38

He went about teaching in synagogues in all the cities and villages. He also continued to demonstrate the use of his talents for helping others find relief from what these people normally had thought was God's punishment. But the more he taught and healed, the more there were who came. He suddenly felt overwhelmed in his efforts to teach everyone and the slowness with which they learned, no matter how sincere their desire to know.

With great compassion, Jesus observed that they were like sheep who were without a shepherd, not knowing how to figure out what to do or where to go until a leader came to show them the way. He also related them to ripe wheat ready for the harvest (their minds ripe to learn), and he said to his disciples, "Pray that God will send laborers into his harvest."

Jesus expands his efforts in order to reach more people.

Matthew 10:1-14

Matthew, who said he was actually there when this occurred, explains that Jesus called his 12 personal disciples to him, saying that he was giving to them the ability to perform spiritual healings and exorcisms. Then he assigned them a mission with policies, procedures, and the boundaries within which they would work.

- Their mission was to preach that the Kingdom of God is already available (as an experience in the mind) and not something in the far distant future.

- Their boundaries and procedure were to stay within the borders of the Tribes of Israel and to heal and perform exorcisms as a part of their work while teaching his message about the Kingdom of Heaven (progressive development of mental/emotional righteousness that leads to direct experience of the beauty that is the Kingdom of God within).

- Their policies were to stay at the home of any helpful person who would give them free lodging as they traveled and to walk quietly away, without condemnation, from the homes of those who had no interest in helping them spread Jesus' message.

Jesus makes predictions.
Matthew 10:16-42

Jesus foretold the indignation and pain his disciples would suffer at the hands of both Romans and Jews. He foresaw the social division among the Jews that would be caused by some believing his message and others disbelieving. He predicted that people in the same household would be turning each other in to the soldiers or putting each other out. Jesus foresaw that eventually the Jews who did not accept his message would be put out of the Holy City of Jerusalem by the Roman oppressors. At that time, his followers would be the only ones permitted to live there. (Historically we know that this did occur many years after Jesus' crucifixion.) He saw that Rome would fall.

Jesus did not say that God will do this, nor did he offer to stop this worldly situation from occurring, or even suggest that he could. He tried to encourage the disciples by saying that not only they, but he also, would experience the same humiliation and abuse just for trying to spread the message of the Kingdom and God's forgiveness. He recommended that as this situation escalated, they should move, when they could, from a city that was persecuting them into one that was not. He said that he would be traveling and spreading the word at the same time and that they would see him again.

Jesus told them to speak openly and bravely of what he had taught them regardless of the threats. He said not to fear that which can kill the body but not the soul. (This establishes that a soul has life in itself, apart from the body, and is something else that does not fit their old belief system. They believed that the soul sleeps in the grave with a dead body, awaiting judgment day when the body will take on flesh again.)

Jesus spoke of the importance of loyalty to one another and said that if they were loyal to him as they communicated with the public, he would be loyal to them as he communicated with God. He also said that if they were afraid to speak in support of him to the public, he would accept their choice by not bringing them to mind as he spoke to God in prayer.

Jesus again challenged the Jewish concept of family involvement as the most important thing to live for. He said that in order to have the strength to support their new beliefs, his disciples must love him even more than their families, because the judgments of their family might make them turn back to the old ideas and deep involvement in family and religion to avoid exclusion. He told the Disciples that they were all to serve the same mission and consistently deliver the same message that he was delivering. The result would be that when listeners heard them, it would be the same as hearing him.

Jesus said that his ideas came from direct communication with God, so that to hear him was to hear ideas from the mind of God.

Then, according to Matthew, Jesus separated from his disciples, and each went into a different area of the mission zone to teach.

Jesus Suggests Progressive Stages of Spiritual Development

In this topic Jesus speaks of entry or initial birth into the kingdom of heaven; the first awareness of the Holy Spirit within. (An birth is a starting point.)

Matthew 11:7-13
Jesus said that John the Baptist was a great man, but that he had not yet been born into the Kingdom of Heaven. He said that even the first birth into spirit makes one greater (through personal experience) than any who have not yet had a spiritual birth.

He said that until now, people have tried to get to the Kingdom of God through violence and thought they could claim the kingdom by war. (That is because they thought the kingdom was earthly territory, the "Promised Land".)

Matthew 11:14
He said that John the Baptist was a reincarnation of Elias, who was prophesied to return (Malachi 4:5.) Elias would return to earth and would be a messenger to prepare people to receive another messenger.

Matthew 11:16-24
Jesus equated their belief (that God will reward them with removal of the human condition) with children sitting in the marketplace saying, in effect, "We have tried to perform our best for you. Now where is our reward?"

He said (to paraphrase), John the Baptist believes in sacrifice, and he obeys all your strict rules of sacrifice. Sacrifice did not bring him freedom from earthly tribulation.

You have put him in prison and condemned him. . ... I do not believe in the sacrifice, and you also condemn me (so sacrifice is not a requirement for God's blessings).

Then Jesus spoke of all the cities in which he had done his work. He had performed *as their prophets had said that he would* with healing miracles and exorcisms. They were willing to accept his miracles, but not his message (to change their beliefs about the nature of God).

Matthew 11:27
Jesus said that only those born into the kingdom of God can know God subjectively, but that others can understand God by accepting the knowledge of God given by one who does know God subjectively. Jesus said that no person can fully know another, but God can fully know anyone who has come to Him.

Jesus pleads with the crowd to release the heavy yoke of religious control.

Matthew 11:28-30

Come. Go my way and take off this heavy labor inflicted on you by the erroneous leaders of your religion . . . I will give you rest. (See Matthew 16:6 for clarification.) "Take my yoke upon you." (A yoke is a guide for leading cattle to water and food. The yoke of the Pharisees was painful and burdensome, indeed, in comparison to the concept of seeking the Kingdom within that was offered by Jesus.) "Learn from me."

Jesus said that mercy, not sacrifice, is the evidence of spiritual righteousness, and that spiritual righteousness (right thinking and right words/action) is what God desires of people.

(Do not confuse righteousness with self-righteousness, which means one who is not able to see his own faults or correct them.)

Next, we will see Jesus making an example of what he meant and the fury that the Pharisees felt in the face of his seeming arrogance.

Religious laws subject to reason in relation to harmlessness

On the Sabbath day, Jesus and his disciples were hungry from their travels and teaching. They did not make the sacrifice of remaining in hunger that was required by their law of the Sabbath. Walking through the corn field, Jesus plucked corn and ate. His disciples did likewise. The Pharisees observed this and challenged him.

Jesus used their scriptures to back up his action, saying there are exceptions to this rule when necessities arise. He used an example of priests breaking the Sabbath in the temple and being held blameless. He defined the cornfield and the world as the temple (that is, nature as the temple) and said that the living person is superior to things of the world.

He said, "If you had understood me when I said I will have mercy and not sacrifice, you would not be condemning me now, for you would understand that those who are the children of God have command even over the Sabbath day." (Notice that when Jesus uses the term "children of"—such as "children of the Pharisees," "my children," or "children of God"—he is referring to those who receive their ideas and guidance from…

Realizing that they simply did not understand that the law of the Sabbath was created in order to require employers and slave owners to give their workers a day of rest from enforced labor, Jesus demonstrated further. He went into the synagogue, and there he healed a man's hand. The healed man was pleased. But this increased the rage of the Pharisees, who were the law keepers of the Jews, and they held a meeting to plan how they might destroy him for teaching the people to break their laws.

Matthew 12:15-16
When Jesus heard about their meeting, he left the synagogue and went about his business. He continued to heal all who came to him, asking them not to tell who had healed them. But they did not honor his request.

(The healing itself was considered an act of defying the Pharisees' teachings because they promoted the idea that illness is a punishment from God. Therefore, illness was required by God as compensation for offending God—the old fear-based Karma concept. This message behind the Pharisees' concern about the healings must not be overlooked when one is attempting to understand the impact of Jesus' ministry upon the Jewish people at that time.)

Matthew 12:24-27

The Pharisees announced that Jesus was using the power of Beelzebub to cast out evil spirits. Jesus responded by saying that was not a rational idea, for how could a power work against itself. If it is *a power*, its very activity would only increase its effects, not eliminate them. *He challenged the people to use reason in their conclusions.*

He also acknowledged that he was not the only person who was practicing casting out evil spirits, saying to the Pharisees, "So whose power do your children (those who learn from you) use to cast out evil spirits?"

He was trying to get them to say that their people were using God's power to cast out evil spirits. This would have been to admit to the listeners that the practice of healing was not an interference with God's punishment, and that others also had power to heal.

Matthew 12:38-40 (repeated in 16:1-4) Pharisees and scribes demanded that Jesus produce a sign from Heaven in order to prove he was in communication with God. He said that the sign of Jonas was the only sign they would get as proof that he was telling the truth. "Jonas was three days and three nights in the belly of the whale. I will be three days and three nights in the heart of the earth."

Jesus says that even the willingness to be *receptive* to greater understanding is more righteous than dogmatism.

Matthew 12:41-42

Jesus gave examples of people in history who had been called unrighteous, asserting that because their minds had been open to accepting greater spiritual wisdom from the wise ones of their day, that the *will to consider other ideas* was evidence that they were righteous in their search for truth. He asserted that the passion to expand one's understanding of God is greater evidence of spiritual righteousness than moral behaviors performed out of fear or an attitude of self-righteousness.

These are the examples he gave:

- The "evil" men of Nineveh believed that Jonas had told the truth after he came back from the belly of the whale. They trusted the report of a person's personal experience and considered it.

- The most corrupt queen of her time traveled great distances to hear the wisdom directly from Solomon. She wanted to learn.

- Jesus said that he is wiser than either Jonas or Solomon, yet they would not accept his report of personal experience, nor would they consider his wisdom about how to broaden their understanding. (A wise person holds to their personal experience, but is willing to reconsider personal interpretation of that experience when some other explanation seems feasible)

Jesus explains why one needs to seek greater understanding.
Matthew 12:43-45

After the development of moral habits has been accomplished in a person, if that person does not understand what is needed next for the development of further spiritual consciousness, he/she will become confused about what to do for further spiritual development. Finding no greater spiritual purpose than morality or *harmless human relations*, he will stop his growth there and eventually cycle back over immersion in the same involvements thus need to relearn lessons he has learned before.

When that happens, he already has a habit of moral actions and finds no opportunities for severe self-discipline. (Developing a habit of moral behavior has been his spiritual goal up until it is accomplished.) Now, without a higher spiritual goal, (understanding the

Plan) *he loses his sense of spiritual passion.* Eventually, out of not knowing there is more than morality to understand, he takes into his mind so many new worldly interests or social or family interests that his vicarious experiences in life will hold even more influences toward evil than it had before morality was developed. (These are diversions from his spiritual path). Instead of understanding, confusion about the contrast between his spiritual consciousness and his attraction or anger with worldly situations and people will arise to fill his thoughts.

Jesus delivers another shocking statement.

Matthew 12:46-50
The Master, Jesus, addressed their concept of the earthly family, which was that

families will rise together in the judgment day and will live together on earth throughout eternity.

He explains that a spiritual family is defined by those who share the same spiritual understanding, (believe and practice the same spiritual understanding) and not by blood or physical lineage.

Defining the Kingdom of Heaven

Jesus was frustrated with the inability of his audience to understand the concept of letting God be King of one's consciousness. He went away seeking solitude in a ship on the shore of the Sea of Galilee. From the ship, he delivered a sermon of several parables about the Kingdom of God (or metaphoric tales about God as the highest authority in one's mind and the importance of correlating one's personal will power with God's Plan).

All of these parables relate to Jesus' warning to his disciples in Matthew 16:6 and to the report from Luke that Jesus said, "the *kingdom o*f heaven is within you." (place of God's authority and guidance)

Luke 17:20-21
Jesus said The Kingdom of God comes not with observation…The Kingdom of God is within you. (God as the ideal of righteousness is sensed in your mind)

Matthew 16:6-12
Attempting to use some of their concepts as a bridge to meet their minds, Jesus warned his disciples to beware of the *leaven* of the Pharisees. This confused them greatly as they could not understand the correlation between the Pharisees and bread. Jesus explained that he is not speaking of bread literally and reminded them of a former parable.

They realized suddenly that Jesus was warning that the ideas taught by Pharisees are like leaven, swelling the former false ideas that are in one's mind. The mind is like bread that is receiving leaven and expanding with the influence and ideas given by the Pharisees.

The parables of heaven

Matthew 13:3-9
Jesus delivered the Parable of the Sower of Seeds. Then he explained privately to his personal disciples that this is not intended to be factual, but it is a story which has a meaning about the planting of ideas and how they grow if they are given attention.

In the next sermon we see him attempting to define the kingdom of heaven by using several parables, one after another, hoping his listeners would get the meaning of at least one of them.

Matthew 13:31-32
Heaven is like a mustard seed. It is the smallest idea planted in the garden of one's mind. Once it takes root (by believing and

using it) then it grows steadily into a great tree.

Matthew 13:33-43

Heaven is like leaven. When accepted as a belief from the teaching of one who knows--or by personal experience--it expands and brings expansion to the mind that receives and considers it.

The disciples follow when he goes into his house, asking him to explain the one about the wheat and the tares. He explains that before purification of the "field" of mind, the false ideas and new ideas grow together until the time to decide (harvest). Then, he gives another parable; one example after another to encourage their understanding.

Matthew 13:44-50

Heaven is like a treasure hid in a field. (The mind discovering knowledge and guidance from the Holy Spirit)

Heaven is like a merchant having sought and found the most valuable pearl. When heaven (the great pearl) is found, the merchant will value it more highly than all his other pearls combined. (pearls as ideas)

Heaven is like a net, having been thrown into the sea. (Sea is the world and people of worldly values) It catches every kind of fish (worldly ideas concerning God) but in the end throws them back.

The "End Time"

When asked when the end time would be, Jesus answered that he did not know, "…only my Father who is in heaven knows".

Shouldn't this answer the question of whether he is God?

Matthew 13:49-52

He explained to *his disciples* that at the "end time of the world" (Jerusalem was their "world") the Jews' occupancy of Jerusalem would end and that he, Jesus, would send angels to offer them comfort. He said there would still be both wicked and righteous people in their world as always and that those who understand and accept the *Kingdom of God* teachings would feel God's presence and not fear that God had cast them out. (Knowing that God is not confined to a city like Jerusalem, they would know that God is with them everywhere, and not feel separated from God)

History tells us that both the stoic Jews and the Romans jointly persecuted the early followers of Jesus, who after a time had become known as Christians.

Later, the Romans turned against only Jews, ousted them from Jerusalem and destroyed their "Holy City" to prevent them from trying to reoccupy it. They were threatened with death if they should try to return. Jerusalem was vacant for some time as the events were compounded.

After time, all Israelites who had openly become followers of Jesus teachings were offered sanctuary. They were permitted to return to Jerusalem, rebuild it and claim it as their holy city. (We see that the Holy City was given to Jesus' followers just as he had said it would be).

The prophets or psychics who predicted a Savior for the Jews had foreseen this, and they had interpreted that idea as the end of the entire world instead of the end of the Jewish "world". These prophets said the vision meant that at the end of the world a judgment day of the dead was coming.

The end of the world interpretation by their prophets had strengthened the Jews belief in ancient Egyptian teachings to which they had been exposed during the hundreds of years they were in Egypt. The Egyptian concept was of a Day of Judgment in which all of the dead would rise from their tombs and take on flesh again, thus the mummification of those who could afford it. It was not a major stretch for the Israelis to add that at the end of the world safety would be offered only to those who accepted the expected Savior as their leader in battle against their enemies. (Jesus referred to the "dead" as those who would not accept the true meaning of Heaven and who thought Heaven was of this world). The interpretation of the Israelis was that those who did not join the followers of the predicted Messiah would be cast out of their "world" to wander in outer darkness. So, we see that prediction being acted out. The ousted Israelis (non-followers of Jesus and his disciples) found they had no place to call their own country. They were in poverty and homeless again as they had been for 40 years after Moses rescued them from Egypt.

Jesus, having psychic foresight of these events, which happened over a period of hundreds of years, was directly addressing the Jews. He was trying to convince Jews to become his followers so they might be included in the group that the Romans would select to occupy Jerusalem after the other events had taken place.

He said to his disciples that a scribe (writer) who has heard these things is like a person with both old and new things in his/her household (household being yet another metaphor to mean the mind).

Matthew 13:54-57

Jesus then went back to his hometown, where he grew up, and taught in the synagogue. But the people who heard him said basically, "Who does he think he's fooling? He couldn't know all these things. He's no one special. He is just the son of the carpenter and his wife. His brothers are James, Joses, Simon, and Judas, and we also know his sisters."

Inability to learn was shown as the result of not being willing to temporarily release existing beliefs in order consider someone else's ideas.

Jesus said, "A man is not without honor except in his own country and among his own family," suggesting that even some members of his own family had ridiculed and doubted him. Matthew reports that Jesus stopped teaching in his hometown after they demonstrated their doubt and only did the healing in an attempt to help open their minds.

The story of John the Baptist's tragedy

Matthew 14:12-22

Matthew reports that when Jesus heard about his cousin John the Baptist being beheaded, Jesus went into solitude in the desert. Here Matthew reports the miracle of the loaves and the fishes, as thousands of people followed him to his hideaway, begging to be healed. In this time of his own grief, compassion for human vulnerability to inconsistent bouts of suffering and joy in this world overwhelmed him, and he did a massive amount of healing work on the spot.

After they had eaten, Jesus told his personal disciples to go to the other side of the Sea of Galilee and wait for him. He said that he would send the people away and then meet the disciples on the other side.

Jesus demonstrates power of prayer, imagery, and the vibrations of the spoken word upon manifestations of nature.

Matthew 14:25-33

According to Matthew, this is when Jesus' personal disciples stopped challenging him against their old beliefs and said to him, "You are the Son of God." (not believing what he said, but accepting because of miracles)

Matthew 14:34-36

After that, Jesus opened his entire spiritual energy. People were enamored with the miracle of the fish and, because of that mind-change from skepticism to faith that illness was not God's will, their beliefs did not block the healing. By believing in the potential, they held a receptive mind. The will to be healed while asking for what they wanted attracted his energy and through the touch of his garments they sensed his energy. Through their own power of belief many were healed

Matthew 15:1-7

Pharisees and the scribes of Jerusalem were outraged at the popularity this man was gaining. In defense of their religion, they saw him as an enemy. They believed he was out to overthrow the religion and take over their temples, rather than a friend who was offering individuals an opportunity to secure their future position in the Holy City. They were determined to find a reason to put him in prison.

Searching for ways to expose him as a rebel against their concept of God's laws, they asked him why he allowed his disciples to eat without washing their hands. Didn't he know this was against the Jewish law?

"You break the rules, too," he responded. "Why do you do it? It's because you are hypocrites." (A hypocrite is one who has different rules for others than for self. Entitled to the advantage because he/she deserves it.)

Jesus Discounts the Benefits of Worshipping Him

Again, denying that he is God.

Matthew 15:7-9

Jesus emphasized that the spiritual path is to have integrity between beliefs and action, to do what you believe is right and to avoid pointing an accusing finger at others who have their own standards.

He used this example: "Some people honor me with words only, saying "believe him", but their true beliefs are far from supporting me. They are hypocrites (not genuine or sincere), and they waste their words. *Some even worship me, but there is no profit in that.* Some teach the rules of men and say that those are the rules of God."

(Good manners and doing things to impress others was taught as Godliness along with many rules about eating and cleanliness)

Jesus delivers a sermon on hand washing, one of Moses' rules, and spiritual righteousness.

Matthew 15:10-11 (Reference 15:1-2)

"It is not what goes into the mouth but what comes out of the mouth that defiles a person."

We cannot speak to anyone else without it being known by God. Speech is an action.

Matthew 15:12-16
The disciples pointed their fingers at the Pharisees, hoping Jesus would notice the look of outrage on the Pharisees' faces and shut down before he got in trouble. Later they said, to paraphrase, "The Pharisees were offended by that last sermon about hand washing. Did you know that?"

The Master responded philosophically, "Every seed becomes a plant. Every tree (full grown idea) that is not developed from a seed of spiritual truth will be uprooted eventually (from the mind). *Let them alone.*

They are blind leaders leading the blind. All of them will fall into a ditch."

Peter said, "Tell us what you meant by the story of being defiled by what comes out of the mouth."

Jesus' weariness and frustration with the dense minds of these people is expressed in his response.

"Are you really that devoid of understanding?" he asked Peter. Then he explained.

Matthew 15:22 through 16:4
A Canaanite woman came asking Jesus to heal her sick child. He did not respond. She pleaded. He explained his Mission, saying that *God had not sent him to teach everyone.* He said he was commissioned to teach only the descendants of Israel, because they were so confused while meaning well, and

because their occupation of the Holy City was also in peril.

She reasoned with him: "If you have the power of God, why can't you use it for everyone?" She was using the same reasoning that he had applied in explaining that if a problem is encountered *you can break a rule if no harm to the other results.* He performed the healing that she requested.

At this point, both the Pharisees and the Sadducees demanded that if he was a representative of God, he must show them a sign from heaven. (They all had the same basic beliefs about God and the purpose for life.) He responded that he found it peculiar that they could look at nature and be logical or discern how one development leads to another. *They could predict what kind of weather or condition might be coming soon, but they could not look in their own holy books and see the learning curve that was predicted for their people through his leadership.*

He refused the challenge to show a sign, saying again that the only sign that they would have was already given in the story of Jonah. This alludes to his coming burial, followed by the Resurrection (coming out of "the belly of the whale" in three days.)

Preexisting Belief System of Jesus' Audience and the Fears that blocked their understanding.

- Acceptance into the group and attachment to the group was all important. One was lost from God's favoritism without that group affiliation. (Ex-communication was always a threat.) Family was all important as a child was an extension of life for the parents.

- Only the Jewish Masters (Jews who have mastered the art of comprehensive reading of the scriptures) could tell you what the scriptures meant. They had been taught as students and scribes, and they all taught the same message.

They believed the ancient Jewish prophets received these messages directly from God, and that those messages applied to all Israelites. If any message was suggested that disagreed with the messages of the prophets, it was blasphemy (an attack against God and the group).

- The descendants of each of the 12 tribes, established in ancient days by the 12 sons of the prophet Israel, were assigned certain lands to inhabit. But in Jesus' day many tribes were living side by side. Still, each tribe had a certain position in the scheme of things for the survival and material advancement of the Jewish people as a whole group. At the time Jesus came, the Jews had been divided into sects. Each sect promoted the same basic historical views, responsibility, and beliefs.

Depending on which prophet they honored the most (even then the messages were less than congruent), they had different concepts about the promised land, the purpose for living, and the rituals and rules by which a Jewish person should live while waiting for Eden to be restored to earth on the Day of Judgment.

- The concept of a day of judgment was absorbed into their culture during their enslavement in Egypt. Moses was raised in Egypt and taught that belief.

- The word heaven was commonly known among all the Jewish sects. The concept of heaven and the events leading to it included the following:

a) Heaven was a place in the sky where God lived. That place would be brought down to earth for faithful Jews to inhabit after the judgment day. Certain events and world changes would have to first take place. No one knew how long it will take except God. The role of the good Jew was to obey the Pharisee priests and live as they dictated while waiting for the judgment day.

b) Only the more well-to-do Jews were educated in reading, and it was believed that only the priests could state the meaning of the scriptures. They believed that the Israelites, who were faithful to the scriptural dictates, would inherit and- in the end times- be the only population on the earth, with no other races around. (A real setup for war) Those who held the Scriptures as supreme truth would enjoy the fruits and products of the earth forever without need for labor. There would be no more enemies to fight for the land and no longer a need to work or to have pain or displeasure of any kind. It was their answer and solution to the questions of "why is there so much pain and trouble in the world along with the moments of happiness and beauty?"

c) The Jews believed that, when this "Eden" was restored, the original sentence for the sin of Adam and Eve would have been served out. They believed the great original sin was copulation. (See the story of Adam and Eve written by Moses as the basic premise from which all other Jewish reasoning and conclusions arose.) They had been taught that God had given a sentence of three punishments to all of Adam's and Eve's descendants (all humanity since Adam and Eve are portrayed as the original human beings from which every race and every person descended). The concept of God was as a tyrannical benefactor who would reward and punish and set dreadful traps for the creatures He had created. He created them as an experiment and for his own amusement, and their role was merely to take care of the beautiful earth He had created.

d)The concept of the three punishments was the Israelites' way of explaining three of the inescapable problems that all humanity faces from generation to generation. Their cry was "when will it end?" Their answer was "on judgment day". That is why they kept asking Jesus when judgment day would come. One proof that he never claimed to be God is his answer, "Only God knows".

The Three Punishments

The Jewish concept of God's three punishments of humanity for falling into the trap of the tree with forbidden fruit and becoming conscious of their nakedness and sexuality are presented here. (Notice the questions addressed and the answers of the Priests per Moses' teachings)

1) Q. Why do men have to labor to survive or earn a living and take care of a wife and little ones?

A. *It is God's punishment of all men for Adam's sin of being seduced into pleasures by a woman:*

Men will labor with great toil and physical effort to get the earth to produce necessities for his survival and to get the goods from the earth. The earth's prolific abundance will now be shut off to human beings, and men will have little time to think about or indulge in their desires because of the need to dig in the ground and tend the animals.

This was the explanation of why men must serve one another in a trade of services. Only men would work in public. The women would have a different form of punishment. The men's punishment was that they could not have what they earned for their own use but must share it with their women and children who, in turn, must act as obedient children toward the man of the family, their benefactor, provider, and protector. (Human family structure was based on this model for centuries, as if it indeed was God ordained.) Even to this date, many men and women carry this concept of responsibility of men to family. Families make unreasonable demands on one another based on these old, co-dependent ideas. It never occurred to these sheep that a man and woman had the right to design their own family structure and agree on roles that were beneficial for all concerned.

2) Q. Why do women have to bear pain in childbirth?

A. *It is God's punishment for Eve and all women after her:*

The first woman had allowed herself to be seduced by the serpent to enjoy that which no person was supposed to enjoy. Subsequently she allowed herself to partake in a second pleasure that she was not supposed to have, specifically sexual pleasure. Her punishment and that of her future descendants was that women would be obligated to endure sexual activity with the man who owned them and would find that this sexual expression was a double-edged sword for them. It would carry only pleasure for the man, but for women it would carry both pleasure and extreme pain— the pain of childbirth.

The woman's punishment was to be the opposite of the man's. He was to be forbidden the comforts of his own home except for a few scant hours each day when he would be too tired to enjoy them. She was to be forbidden the enjoyment of freedom to leave the home except on rare occasions, as her burden of labor in the home would keep her busy day and night. In addition to that, she would have a different kind of labor. No more would God create human beings out of the earth, but they would grow inside the body of the woman and come forth with great pain to her. Then she would be further restricted from outside adventures, as the children would be hers to look after and teach. Marriage was sanctified by God as the only right under which people could indulge in sexual pleasures. Anyone who indulged in sexual activity outside of marriage was breaking God's law by ignoring His requirement for marriage as the only avenue through which God's favored children, the Hebrews (later to be known as Israelites), were to be born into the earth.

A child born of parents who were not married to one another was considered to be not of God, an outcast. A man could have as many wives and children as he could afford. With his labor he must provide for them. A woman was the possession of a man, and therefore, she could not belong to more than one man. She would go from being provided for by her father to being provided for by her husband and the father would be free from responsibility to her. To have a girl child was to have a burden of responsibility, as the girl was not expected to grow up and provide for herself. Her father would have the gloomy responsibility of protecting her chastity and saving up a dowry to be given the man she would marry. The dowry would make it easier to transfer responsibility from one man to another. Marriage was considered the basis of the small group, and every family member had specific roles to play for both present and future involvement in family care. To produce and raise children was the purpose for marriage. If one could not get pregnant or impregnate, it was considered a punishment by God. Divorce was forbidden, and in those days a woman was not allowed to work in society, only in the home of a man. Women were looked upon as weak people with a valid dependency because of this role. If a man divorced a woman and put her out of his home, her only options for survival after divorce were begging or prostitution.

3) Q. Where did all the people who are "non-Hebrew" come from? Why is there animosity between us and them? How did Hebrews get to be the Chosen People of God?

A. Jewish scriptures (Old Testament) stated that God's punishment of the people also carried the potential for ex-communication.

With this, the Jewish, and later the early Christian, practice of ex-communication is justified. Plus, we see justice by punishment, imprisonment and public records of crimes being carried out in our present-day society.

The second phase of the Hebrew's story of the world's beginning, as written by Moses, states that Cain and all his descendants were *banished* from the opportunity to belong to the Chosen Tribes or associate with them.

The idea of home life was depicted as Adam toiling outside the comfort of the home that he had worked to build (his original sin punishment), while Eve toiled away inside the home with no time to rest and enjoy the home, producing children as a direct consequence of copulation with a man (her original sin punishment). The prolific garden of Eden had become the societal place of delegated duties and struggle for survival, so what more was there to lose?

The Hebrew's story of life states that when Cain saw his brother as competition, he killed his brother out of jealousy. That became the cause of death in the world. God then taught Cain, through ex-communication from the Garden of Eden and the association with his tribe, that cooperation and acceptance of duties were required in order to expect the benefits of living within a society. The opportunity to be a part of the social structure of a group was only for those who cooperated, accepting their roles without defiance. As a result of Cain's act of violence and his efforts to deceive God, the story says that God cast him out of his familiar environment and out of association with those of his own culture.

Ex-communication from the inhabitants of Eden was not only Cain's punishment, but the punishment of all his descendants. Cain's descendants are all non-Hebrews, the ones ex-communicated from God. Now Cain would no longer work at easily assigned jobs but would experience the need for survival as a competitive struggle. If he could survive among the others, he would always have to watch his back in case they wanted to give to him what he had given to his brother: jealousy, death, and pain. They would distrust him for no reason other than they knew he was a descendent of God's Chosen people, and was not of their culture. (Note that the story did not attempt to give any explanation as to where the others came from or what their identity was.)

Fear of being ostracized from the group became a core concern for the Hebrews based on this bit of their history. Great emphasis was placed on obedience, humility, sacrifice, attention to duty and devotion to family in order to prove dedication. This fear of ex-communication became the Israelis' major deterrent from willingness to accept Jesus' teachings.

These stories were passed down to Hebrews from generation to generation. The writer of Genesis promoted them as literal facts and stated that God would punish anyone who altered these stories or caused them to be forgotten or lost. The stories were said to be written by God, and the Hebrews used them as the answer to where they came from, who they were, what their relationship to the creator of the world was, and what they could expect from God in the future. The most commonly accepted belief among Biblical scholars is as formerly stated, that these stories were first written by Moses so the Israelites would understand their culture and their identity as the Chosen People of God. Moses did not promote the concept of one God, but of one major God—the Hebrew God—and many lesser gods of other nations. He promoted the view that the Hebrew God was jealous of his people, that He required total loyalty to Him and that the Hebrew God was more powerful than the other gods.

These, then, were the fears and beliefs of Jesus' audience, the people he came to enlighten with a true concept of the nature of

God, forgiving, loving, non-punishing and tolerant.

Fearing the loss of acceptance within the Jewish society and the synagogue, Jesus' audience wanted more than anything to cooperate with the rules in order to avoid bringing further punishments to themselves, their people, their children, and their children's children. They hoped to be judged as cooperative enough in the long run to have their original garden restored to them. After the restoration, they would have no enemies, no rebels, no work, no pain, and no non-Jews to deal with. At the point of the "end time of punishment," all childbearing would stop. The bones of all the Hebrews who had ever lived and were now sleeping would come out of the graves, be given flesh bodies again, and judged. All those judged cooperative and subservient enough to live in Eden would be allowed to stay on the earth. Others would be cast off the earth into the darkness (of outer space). Those staying on the earth would live forever in the restored Garden of Eden. Death would have been abolished along with childbearing, pain, and work. There would be only prolific abundance, peace, and freedom to play, eat, dance, and sing. There would be no responsibilities for anyone, just as it was in the beginning. This was their concept of heaven and the afterlife.

Some sects believed they would have physical bodies while others said no, that God would make a new kind of body for the inhabitants of Eden. It would be made of a new substance, and that new substance would never wear out or have pain, illness, or death. The new earth and everything in it would be made of that same substance. Some had heard from the heathen societies, such as Grecian and Egyptian, the myth of an evil one called Satan who was struggling with God for the loyalty of human beings, and that those who accepted the gifts of Satan would have an afterlife of burning in hell forever. Moses accounts alluded to such ideas.

The Israelites (a name coined by one Hebrew and his family who separated willingly from the main body of the Hebrews because of their disobedience to God) were well-meaning people who wanted to do what was right and obey God's law. But until Moses gave them the rules of conduct for a cooperative society, they could only guess at what was righteous in the sight of God.

Because they believed that all difficulties in life were direct punishments by God, they perceived their situations such as illness, famines, floods, defeats in war, and having to live as servants or second-class citizens in some other nation's territory to be God punishing them. They perceived their health, prosperity, having their own land and authority over themselves as God's reward to them. The ancestors of Jesus' audience had believed and passed on the belief from generation to generation that if they, as a group, would obey Moses' social laws to the letter, then they could make some progress instead of being punished all the time. They felt that eventually God would forgive them for the sins of Adam, Eve, and Cain and for all their poor judgments and blatant sins. Until then, if even one disobeyed, the whole group was punished by God, just as in the beginning. From this premise, they assumed that they were obligated to edit one another's behaviors and to chastise or judge and cast out one another.

As the years went by, more health rules and rules about human relations were added as laws. Extensive rules were made about how often to pray for the release of the Hebrew people. Rules were made to require the people to sacrifice certain pleasures and possessions for demonstrating their willingness to give up everything for God's approval. There were rules about the necessity of giving part of one's goods to God through bringing vegetables or prized animals to the synagogue as a representation of the willingness to sacrifice in order to gain God's approval. The lawgivers, priests, and scribes ate well.

Eventually rituals were increased, all with the hope that Eden would soon be restored if they sacrificed enough. The name of the expected reward had been changed from Eden to heaven. The ritualistic, formal sacrifice was a scapegoat. This annual scapegoat offering was a symbolic representation of the group's begging for forgiveness and release from having to pay for the sins of Adam and Eve. It was a genuine cry for relief from all that made their lives difficult and a promise that if they could just start over, they would not break God's rules again.

The common belief of the Israelites was that, before Eden could be restored, certain things would happen. These things had been told the Hebrew people by psychics (prophets) and astrologers of various generations. (Those predictions are given in the books about the various prophets that are found in the Jewish scriptures, called the Old Testament.) These psychic views of future events were basically true, but the error was in believing that God was deliberately making it happen rather than letting it happen through nature, social trends, their own choices, and the choices of other people in the earth. They had no understanding of natural law or social trends and their effect on matters of human psychology. They also had no understanding of the effect that one person's ideas could have upon the mind of a person who was not thinking for himself. This made it easy for them to let someone else think for them, as if they were blameless if they did not use their own minds to govern their journey through life.

The predictions were that there would first be many generations of oppressed Israelites similar to the times before Moses. They would have no nation or geographical territory of their own but would have to set up housekeeping in the territories of other nations and submit to the rules of those nations as well as be treated like unwelcome visitors in the lands of their habitation. When Jesus arrived on the scene, social and political trends had brought them to that position as residents within the great Roman Empire. It was the story of Cain played out in mass. They would suffer great indignities under the rule of these people and be suppressed and oppressed for their own preferred way of living.

They believed that after these things had come about, then God would send a rescuer to save the Israelites, His Chosen people. This rescuer would be a warrior, and he would kill oppressors (Cain's descendants) by leading the Israelite tribes in a war they could not lose. God would now, at last, be on their side to give them great strength and power for defeating their enemies. No one would be able to stand against this great rescuer, who would come to fight for their freedom and the restoration of Eden to the Jews; God's chosen people. He would also be their teacher of righteousness.

Once this battle was over and they had defeated their oppressors, some of the oppressors would be dead, and others would be merely captured. Those oppressors would have a chance to convert and to join the society of the chosen. Those who refused would eventually receive the most horrible of punishments from God. For a thousand years, all the oppressors would be imprisoned, and with them Satan would be imprisoned and chained for a thousand years. Peace then would reign in this cooperative society, proving that they had pleased God and his angels.

After a millennium, Satan would break loose from his chains and roam the earth again, influencing the people to do evil things and to defy God. A great and bloody battle between the armed forces of good and the armed forces of evil would follow. The rescuer/savior/messiah would come back and lead the battle for the good forces, and they would win again.

All the evil ones, including Satan, would be (according to the belief of some of the sects) cast off the earth into the darkness of space, where they would remain conscious forever, suffering from fear, remorse, and deprivation of the good things of earth for all eternity with no more chances to change their ways.

In the belief of other sects, Satan (the outcast angel Lucifer) would be sent back to the universal territory that God had assigned him in the beginning when he first began to break the rules of cooperation (just like Cain had done). The name of this place that was given to Lucifer is hell, and it is made of a substance that is filled with the hottest fire imaginable. Lucifer will be the ruler there. He will influence the people in hell to do all kinds of horrible things to each other in an environment that scorches their skins day and night. There will be not a moment of escape from the torture, the fear, the physical pain, and anxiety. There will be no further opportunity for changing one's ways.

The next step in establishing this Heaven on earth, after Lucifer has received all the judged living people, will be that God will tell all the bones in the ground and in the sea and in the caskets and tombs to rise up and to come to one place, the place of judgment. When all the bones have risen and are lined up for judgment, they will be free from group judgment and will receive individual judgment for their own behaviors while they were alive. This individual judgment will determine whether they stay in Eden or are cast off (into outer darkness OR into a burning hell). The judgment of those living on the earth at that time would have already taken place through the result of the battle itself. Those who lost the battle by refusing to cooperate were to be the losers and go straight to hell.

Their belief was that none other than the expected rescuer/savior/messiah would be making the judgment on that great judgment day. He would sit on a throne and would pronounce earth as his kingdom. He would be the King of the Jews and of all those who had cooperated with them. Anyone that he judged as unworthy to live in his kingdom would be thrown off the earth. Others would stay and share the good things: the abundance and pleasures of earth and the pleasures of socializing with one another. He would then reign as king of the Earth forever and they would never see trouble again because he would be their God and would tell them clearly what to do. They would obey him with gratitude for their salvation from Satan's (the Serpent's) influence and the hell it could have brought. All will be like children, playing and having pleasure in a protected environment with no responsibilities except to praise the Savior.

Examination of the gospels continues.

In the early part of Jesus' ministry, we saw him working to gain an audience with the use of two impressive skills:

1) Building a bridge between his own premises and those of his audience

by demonstrating knowledge of their beliefs and then interpreting those beliefs according to more idealistic and abstract views.

2) Manipulation of energy: altering the beliefs held in mind to produce healings, both physical and mental, and to produce unexplained phenomenon.

Later, after that audience had been attracted, he began to demonstrate the harmlessness of breaking some of their religious rules, not only the ones made in more recent days but even ones that were given by Moses, whom they considered to be the infallible lawgiver. Jesus openly stated that a living soul is superior to the laws under which he/she serves, and that the law of the Sabbath is not a law about righteousness. It is a law meant to provide for the people an opportunity to rest, established at a time when they had been enslaved and forced to work all of their waking hours. The result of his explanation was a greater rift between his supporters and opposers.

Indeed, he did bring a sword to separate individuals from the mass thinking. He encouraged people to think for themselves, and he did not bring peace. In an effort to wake them up to the need for establishing their own personal relationship with God through private inner communication with the Holy Spirit, we see him stepping out into increasingly stronger stands for what he knows to be true.

The Rock

Testing the disciples' capacity to understand, Jesus asked Peter's opinion about his identity. When Peter acknowledged without hesitation that he knew Jesus to be the Messiah they had been expecting, Jesus confirmed that belief by saying this would be the rock upon which he would build his church. This phrase is used as yet another metaphor but has been interpreted as meaning that Peter is as solid as a rock, and that Jesus will build his church through Peter. However, in the very next conversation we see him calling Peter "Satan."

Could it be that the rock he referred to was the knowledge itself—the knowledge that Jesus was the Spiritual Leader sent by God to the Jewish people—rather than meaning that Peter the man was a rock? And could the word church mean an inner religious structure or belief system built upon that idea?

Certainly, if one starts with the premise that Jesus was a spiritual leader sent by God, one can build a mental religious structure upon that premise which would include only what he taught about righteousness, the nature of God, the potential of the individual who believes, and the position of the kingdom of heaven.

If Jesus could get his listeners to build this new belief system and act on it, then it would eventually expand to the point of replacing/displacing the former religious structure or religious belief system in their minds and save them from stagnation in their spiritual growth. It would open their minds to the possibility of individual communion with God.

Keys to the Kingdom

Using yet another simile, Jesus announces that he will give to Peter the keys to the kingdom of heaven (tell him what the keys are).

Jesus addresses the concept of thoughts held in mind.

Matthew 16:19

The keys open the door of the mind that lead to one's experience of the holy place within, a place in the mind that is free from vengeance, hatred, etc., and a place where one has only peaceful, lovely, idealistic thoughts and experiences. (A key is an instrument which turns the lock so a door can be opened. In this case, their belief of a punishing God formed a locked door in the minds of people.)

The keys that he presented

Key #1. Whatever you tie up and hold on earth will also be tied up and held in (your) heaven, or spiritual consciousness (emotional cause and effect of harboring vengeful ideas).

Key #2. Whatever you let go of on earth will also be set free from heaven, (from your thinking).

Later he gave these *keys* to all his disciples by repeating them as stated to Peter.

Naively the early Christians taught and believed that he had said Peter would literally be in charge of who could go into Heaven and who would be kept out. They thought he meant that Peter would be the final judge, sorting people out for God. (The early Christian church was founded upon that literal premise of Peter and his descendants and appointed leaders as the keepers of the keys, saying who could enter heaven or not.)

The Jews considered heaven to be an Earthly place that would be their eternal home after the judgment day. When the followers of Jesus and his disciples were left to interpret his sayings for themselves, they took on two beliefs: 1.) Heaven was an earth-type place in the sky that the soul would inhabit after death if it admitted that Jesus was God. 2.) At the end of the world, great wars would occur; all the non-Christians would be cast off the world, and Jesus would return to rule the entire world with Christians as his subjects. The world would be restored to its Eden-like condition with no work required, and only Christians would occupy the world.

Those who preferred the belief that Peter was to be the infallible representative of God formed common groups. Those who preferred the belief that Jesus would come back some day and judge the world's people, destroying those who had not accepted him, formed their own groups. Most of the Christians accepted both theories. Even after all the parables stating the nature of the kingdom of heaven, they still had not understood. The later establishment of the Catholic Church by Christ's followers and the idea of the pope being a direct descendant of Peter and in charge of who could go to heaven was based on this misunderstanding.

They also assumed that the word paradise and the phrase eternal life were synonymous with each other and with the word Heaven. Later, we will see that Jesus specifically defines what he means when he says life, and that he never uses the word Paradise as a synonym for the word heaven.

After telling Peter what the keys are, Jesus requested that his disciples let him keep a low profile for a time by keeping his identity quiet in order to give him some time.

He began to prepare them for the abuse he would endure when they entered Jerusalem. He explained that he would suffer humiliation and be killed. He said that his plan was to arise on the third day from the very state of death. (If it proved necessary for getting his point across, he was willing to suffer this inevitable experience. It would come as a result of his speaking openly. If the arrest and conviction were to come, he would use it to his advantage by demonstrating that life is in the soul; that it is the soul that brings life to a body, and that the individuality of a person survives after leaving the body.)

Peter failed to realize that Jesus was explaining his plan. He believed that Jesus was complaining about what would happen to him and asking for help. Peter perceived the concern about Jesus' safety as a problem that he, himself, must try to prevent.

Peter insisted that he would defend his friend and would not allow this to happen. But Jesus very sternly demanded the cooperation of all his disciples in this matter. In order to carry out the role of the spiritual teacher as presented in the ancient scriptures (so more people would believe his teachings), it was his plan to follow the script, submit to arrest, and face the possibility of crucifixion. They must not interfere.

He said that those who would stay with him now were likely to receive the same treatment, but they also would be alive, not dead, and would go to live in an actual place where he would also be residing, a place that he called not heaven but paradise.

The disciples get serious about trying to learn from him.

Matthew 18:1

Who is the greatest in heaven? (They are again confusing his talk of paradise, a universal realm that he will inhabit after leaving the earth, with the concept of heaven, a place of righteousness and spiritual beauty in the mind.)

Matthew 18:3

Jesus used the inquiring mind and receptivity of a child as an example of how to get into that inner beauty that he said is heaven, saying that a person cannot even make the initial entry into heaven (the place of spiritual idealism and wisdom within) unless they first be converted and become as a little child: (inquiring, curious, receptive to new ideas, enthusiastic about exploring spirituality)

Matthew 18:7-10

He explains the importance of not trespassing, ignoring another's boundaries or getting into another person's space without permission, or trying to interfere with the direction another is going. He says it is natural that people will have pain and sorrow in the world but warns them not to be guilty of deliberately being a source of pain and emotional sorrow for another person. Again, he uses very outrageous exaggerations to try to get his point across.

He suggests that if tempted to bring physical pain or injury to another, a person must discipline self against it.

He says again that he came to save those who are lost (confused, going around in circles, don't know how to get where they want to go spiritually).

Jesus offers a formula for handling those who offend us

Matthew 18:15-17

This can also be understood as those who ignore your boundaries or get into or stay in your physical or mental space against your will. This was his suggested alternative to their traditional vengeance. Vengeance was considered by the listeners to be spiritual justice.

1) Go and tell her/him privately about the problem. If she/he will address it rationally with you, then peace can be restored between you. (First try to work it out personally and privately.) The goal is to restore peace.

2) If the person will not reason with you, then discuss it with that person in front of a few witnesses so they can offer their objective opinion when listening to both opinions.

3) If she/he still will not cooperate, then tell it to the church and let them decide by the church laws what is right.

4) If this still does not produce cooperation, then stop your involvement and your communication with that person. Ex-communicate them from your thoughts. (Later we see Jesus

demonstrating this by unresponsiveness during his trial and crucifixion.)

Matthew 18:18

The keys to heaven are repeated, clearly showing that it is one's worldly ideas plus their spiritual ideas that occupy the mind, and that these ideas stay in the soul until altered by you. If the worldly ideas and the spiritual ideals are not compatible, Jesus suggests letting go of those beliefs and habits that are in conflict with one's spiritual ideals of what is righteous. (The keys to heaven are given as concepts that one needs to know and practice.)

1) Whatever you are attached to in the world will also be in Heaven (Your mind).

2) Whatever you release back to the world (refuse to interact with) will not be active in your heaven. (mind)

Matthew 18:21-22

Peter did not know that letting go (releasing involvement with something, whether thought, verbal, or physical involvement) is, in itself, an act of forgiveness or release. Jesus emphasized that releasing begins in the mind. The need for retribution, or payback, had been a major focus of the Israelite's religious history and training, and the demand for retribution had been a major focus of their concept of justice. This idea of releasing is startling to them.

Their concept of forgiveness meant to subject oneself again by requiring them to admit wrong and accept their punishment. Releasing as a means of forgiveness, or setting free, was a totally new concept to this group of listeners.

Pondering the idea Peter asked a question. "How often must I forgive? Seven times?"

Jesus used his abstract style of response again, "No, seventy times seven." (He means that every time someone offends you, just address it gently or let it go so that it will not affect your emotional nature and build up resentment in your mind.)

Jesus attempted again to explain that the kingdom of heaven is in the mind. When one gets rid of the clutter of holding onto past hurts and greed and trying to be repaid with apologies, money, subservience, services, or other types of retributions for abuse, the pearl of great price can be found with its spiritual qualities and spiritual powers inside the individual's mind.

Jesus attempts to explain another parable

Matthew 18:23-35

The Kingdom of Heaven can be understood through this story. A king loaned money to his servants and kept an account of what they owed him. One owed 10,000 large coins but had no way to pay, and the king, being business-minded, said the person would need to accept the consequences of his default on the loan. But the servant begged for mercy and more time. The king felt compassion for the offender and forgave him the debt. (released him from retribution)

Having accepted forgiveness and freedom from the one he begged for mercy, this same servant had no empathy for a fellow servant who had borrowed from him and asked for more time. He had his debtor bound and imprisoned.

It is only the unforgiving mind that holds onto its grudges and a desire to punish sense the offender. A person cannot come into spiritual freedom until he/she lets go of wanting to force compensation from others. Releasing the offender with no debts to repay is fair. But deliberate punishment of the offender is a refusal to give what every person would desire from another, forgiveness, and mercy.

Jesus said that heaven is within you, a part of your consciousness. If so, then its' opposite experience, hell, must also be within the mind that dwells in thoughts of getting even or in fear of letting go of a person or situation who is stimulating the vengeful, emotional ideas in you.

Separating from the offender and releasing thoughts of the offense is to claim one's own freedom while setting the other free as well. Pursuing the offender and demanding a pay-back is emotional imprisonment for both.

Pharisees Question Jesus

In order to have more supporters in their plot to get rid of him, the Pharisees question Jesus in relation to their laws of justice or righteousness. The Pharisees asked for Jesus' opinion about the law of divorce as given by Moses.

You will recall that in that culture a woman was a dependent all her life, like a child who never grew up. And the custom was that a man was required to work and earn money to support his entire household and every person in it because they were his belongings and not expected to earn money for their own livelihood.

There was no opportunity in that society for a woman to earn money and support herself except as a prostitute. In that society, a woman that no man wanted to keep had no choice but to beg or to become a prostitute. There was no question about whether a woman ought to divorce her husband, because if she did, she would have no place to go and would have to become a prostitute or a beggar. There were no work/study programs, free education programs, or welfare programs as in today's world. There was no potential for a female to get a job or for a government agency to assist the untrained citizens as in today's society of self-responsibility.

Knowing all this about them, Jesus did not suggest restructuring their society. This would have been too radical and premature for this consciousness of people. Instead, he stated what would be merciful within the context of such a culture. He showed again, through his message, that there are no behavioral absolutes of right or wrong; behaviors affect people, not God. Therefore, it is a human relations issue within the context of a societal structure.

In such a society as this, he said that unless a woman were to make herself an adulteress by breaking her fidelity vows, a man should not force her into such a life by divorcing her. The disciples contemplated what he had said and responded, in effect, "Well if that's the case, then marriage removes a person's options for ever being free again or for changing partners. It would be better for a man if he did not marry at all, wouldn't it?"

To answer yes to this would have been to offend *their sense of purpose for life,* which was to perpetuate the race through marriage and producing children and grandchildren, etc. Jesus answered that whether a person chooses to marry is not a question of righteousness. It is a choice based on the nature of the man and his purpose for marriage or not marriage. His reply was that each man should make his own decision about whether to marry, but the choice comes with responsibilities.

Eternal Life

A refreshing question not about human relations but about eternal life arises. (In John 17:3, Jesus defines life as knowledge of God.)

Matthew 19:16-30
"Good Master, what good thing must I do to have eternal life?"

Before answering, Jesus emphatically states that he is not God. (**Matthew 19:17**)

(Obviously this was more important than the answer to the question.)

Jesus starts with the basics

Answer: "Obey the laws of moral behavior if you want knowledge of God (eternal life)."

Response: "I've been doing that all my life, so what else can I do?"

Jesus said, "Well, if you're talking about more abundant life than just a moral character can bring, make the pursuit of greater knowledge of God your only goal and treasure. Release, from your thoughts and from your path, everything and everyone that holds you back or takes your time from following the spiritual path."

He was a rich man who had worked hard for what he had and was not willing to abandon his material treasures to seek greater spiritual realization.

Easier for a camel to go through the eye of a needle

Jesus did not condemn the man, nor did he say that God would condemn him. He merely remarked that a person has freedom to seek personal knowledge of God. When one is not willing to let go of dwelling on whatever is interfering with that pursuit the person is deliberately letting those things or people take the mind away from the intent to experience "heaven".

What keeps one from making free choices is attachment to things, intrigue with the lives of other people, activities, worldly situations, opportunities for financial reward or public acclaim, personal pleasures, and personal responsibilities. The primary detriment to freedom is the hunger for material wealth and the concern for losing it after it is gained. Such a person would have a difficult time developing greater knowledge of God because other things are more prominent in the mind.

Jesus' disciples were amazed at this concept, because in their culture, wealth and possessions were viewed as signs of having pleased God.

"Who, then, can be saved?" they asked.

Jesus answered that a man without knowledge of God (life) cannot be saved from ignorance of God (death). This is self-evident since knowledge cancels out ignorance, and ignorance precedes knowledge. Therefore "death", or lack of knowing God comes before "life" (knowing God) and not the other way around. Think about it.

Peter inquired about what kind of benefit he and the other disciples had earned by letting go of their other interests and following Christ.

"We all did that. We left everything and followed you in order to know more about God. What will we have for that?" (Please remember that Jesus has already stated emphatically that he is not God.)

Paraphrased answer: "When you come to the *place where I will be residing* after my regeneration (paradise, an environmental dimension in the universe), you will have freedom and creative power.

Everyone who has to let go of friends and family and worldly things in order to follow me will have much more of value there than anything they have let go of here on earth. But in the stormy times now approaching, *we* will go through a great deal of tribulation and pain on the earth. What you get for accepting the knowledge is the knowledge itself."

What you do with the knowledge is your choice. Every choice has its own responsibility.

He cautioned the disciples not to think they should have greater benefits in the spiritual realms than others who might come later (parable of the penny for work and of the prodigal son). He suggested that the desirable attitude is to celebrate that everyone who accepts the knowledge of the Holy Spirit receives the same benefit: the joy, confidence and peace in knowing God more fully. You either accept the freedom to seek that knowledge, or you don't. It is a choice.

Matthew 20:18

He reminds the disciples of his plan and what will happen to him and that he will be regenerated on the third day.

CHAPTER FOUR

Jesus as a Ransom

Kidnapped party: one who is held captive

The Jewish philosophy was that the children of Israel were being kept from their freedom by the original sin of Adam and Eve and were being forced by God to pay back through pain and suffering until God felt they had suffered enough. No one could know how long it might be before God would set them free. Jesus saw them as captives, also, but captives of their religious beliefs, especially that of an original sin that resulted in God's punishment of all humanity. Repeatedly we see Jesus' quarrel being with the Pharisees, not with the Romans.

Kidnapper: one who holds someone captive and not free

The Jews' belief was that God had taken away their freedom and required great sacrifices from them.

Ransom: that which is traded to set the captive party free

The concept of the mystical order of the Jews, the Essenes, was that a wisdom teacher would come to set them free by bringing them a greater understanding of the truth; knowing the truth would set them free. But the mainstream majority of the Jews believed that eventually God would take pity on them for their efforts to please Him and send a rescuer to destroy their oppressors and restore Eden to them, just as it was before the original sin. Because they could not be perfect, they believed their offenses to God continued to multiply, causing further indebtedness and need for greater retribution. They felt they would never get out of debt to God unless He would feel sorry for them and send the rescuer (Messiah).

For those who were not capable of understanding either the truth about new beliefs or the truth of God and eternal life, the symbolism of a Messiah to come was taken literally by the Israelites. Their belief system was that if they as a group practiced the moral codes and all the other hundreds of restricting laws for an indeterminate period of time, and if they obeyed the church leaders fully, and if they prayed and sacrificed and begged for forgiveness for the sins of Adam and Eve and of all their forefathers long enough, eventually God would reward them for their efforts by sending a messiah (savior) to lead them in a great battle to win their freedom from their oppressors. So the people were taught that they could not be saved from sin until this messiah came. The only way they would accept that they were free from God's wrath was to believe that the Messiah had come. There was no use in petitioning God for their own salvation from sin because the story said that they would all be saved at the same time, when God decided they had suffered enough as a group. (The catch was they certainly did not know that their oppressors were the leaders of their religion.)

SCAPEGOAT: A SUBSTITUTE TO SACRIFICE FOR THE REAL OFFENDER

Actual goats were offered to God as sacrifices to buy some degree of temporary forgiveness for their sins until the real scapegoat, the Messiah, were to come to them. Then he would be the final scapegoat, and they would be forgiven forever.

As the expected messiah or wisdom teacher, Jesus wanted to influence them to let go of their belief that they were condemned. For the sake of those who believed that their freedom would come through learning spiritual truth from the wisdom teacher, he taught of the forgiving nature of God, that righteousness begins with a way of thinking and feeling, that the kingdom of heaven is available to everyone, and that the Holy Spirit with knowledge of God can be experienced in their own minds. But in order to influence the literal thinkers to let go of the old belief and accept forgiveness, he would need to follow the script written by Israel and other psychics throughout Jewish history. These psychics (prophets) had seen images of the future, glimpses of this very time, and had written them down as a way that the Israelites could recognize the rescuer when he came.

In order to convince them that they were free, Jesus would need to follow that script as precisely as possible, thus acting out what they perceived the required ransom to be, a savior to suffer in their place as the scapegoat for all descendants of Israel.

Of course, Jesus knew they were in bondage not to God but to this belief system. He was indeed sent by God to free them from that belief system. The actual coin of exchange was not the person, but the new belief system sent to them. The new belief system offered by him would set this race of people free from their fear of God. Getting them to accept it was his work to do.

The actual kidnappers and keepers of the prison gate were the Jewish scribes and Pharisees. They refused to accept the true ransom, new life-giving beliefs in exchange for the old fear-driven beliefs. They attacked the messenger, as if to kill him would be to kill his coin of exchange.

But his intent and his action were to make the exchange in form as well as symbolically. This way, even those who would not let go of the old belief until someone paid the price that they thought was required would have a chance to be set free from their self-made mental prison.

So, Jesus permitted the concept of a gross (actual) ransom to be played out in order to help free them from their false beliefs that God was punishing them.

Three Types of Audience

Israelites could have one of three different mind-sets concerning the issues that Jesus addressed. His messages and activity would give each type an opportunity to gain belief in freedom from the ancient teachings about their people being punished by God for the "sins" of Adam and Eve.

The first type of audience would comprehend his message about stagnant beliefs being the thing that keeps one from advancing into a new realization of God. This group would have understood and accepted his message about the true nature of God, and about the soul's true relationship to God. If all his listeners and followers had understood these things just from hearing them, he would not have had to go farther. But there were others who desired understanding yet had no capacity to understand his abstract message.

The second type of audience was made up of those willing to believe him but afraid to release the idea of needing to offer retribution to God. They were morally developed but still incapable of understanding abstract ideas. They could be convinced to change their beliefs only if they witnessed proof for themselves. These were the ones who would observe and listen and determine his credibility by comparing his life to the predictions in their scriptures. If they could witness the predictions being fulfilled, they would believe he was the Messiah they had expected and that they were now free from the required retribution for the original sin of Adam and Eve. They wanted to believe that they were accountable only for their own errors, but they needed to feel that redemption had taken place in order to accept their freedom.

Again, in their belief system designed by earlier Israelites and carried on for generation after generation, the scapegoat or sacrificial lamb was an exchange for their freedom from paying for the original sin (a symbolic ransom to God). The analogy of himself as a sacrificial lamb that God had sent as a free gift to them was not believable to them unless that sacrificial lamb suffered and was killed. That is why he referred to himself as the lamb. It was for the ears of this group so that they might believe and accept their freedom from God's punishment. How could they know that the Messiah's actual sacrifice had been to leave his paradise in order to perform this mission? The mission was an assignment to teach Israelites the truth about the nature of God and an individual's relationship to God through the Holy Spirit.

The third type of audience that he wanted to convince was also made up of Israelites who did not comprehend the message concerning change of beliefs. However, they were intrigued by his saying that souls do not stay in the grave with the body but go on to live somewhere else. Wanting to believe that, and watching to see, they would believe only after hearing witnesses say that he had not actually died, even though he had suffered apparent death. In order to assure the releasing of their belief in the whole concept of judgment day and sleeping corpses in the graves, he would need to literally face physical death and then demonstrate that he was still able to think—and communicate—as a living being not sleeping in a tomb in wait for a judgment day.

Having done his work with group number one, Jesus then rushed into the next phase of his ministry that was needed for convincing groups two and three. These were the strong believers of the religious view, who would lift their own chains of eternal waiting and self-condemnation only if they were convinced that God had made a reciprocal exchange as a sign of his forgiveness and love for them. The reciprocal exchange must be God's greatest prize, just as their scapegoat gifts to God had been their most prized possessions of produce, money, and animals. The lamb sacrificed to them by God would be His son. Let us consider what Matthew said about it.

CHAPTER FIVE

The Great Pre-Planned Drama Begins

Jesus and his twelve personal disciples went to a place called the Mount of Olives from where he sent two of his friends into the village to get a pair of animals, a donkey, and her colt. He told them where the animals would be and that they need only tell the owner that their lord (a word for employer in those days) had need of the animals, as if he had prearranged it with the owner.

This whole drama was needed in order to reach people of mind-sets two and three. He knew they might be tracking his validity by reading the ancient prophecies, which predicted that he would arrive on a donkey. Many people, then believing that he was indeed the ransom promised to the Jews still thought it would be a people to people battle he would be leading them in instead of a battle of beliefs against beliefs.

They followed him in procession, creating a roadway with garments they threw on the path and palm branches that they cut down. This was a way of treating him like royalty. The messiah had been expected to be a descendant of the blood line of King David, who had sung songs about a messiah (savior) who was to come. They chanted "Hosanna to the son of David" as a sign of their belief that he was the one they had been expecting.

Citizens of Jerusalem saw him with the parade of people coming and said, "Who is that?" The crowd answered, "It is Jesus, the prophet from Nazareth, of Galilee."

Matthew reports that the first thing Jesus did after arriving in the city was to show his offense at the practice of using the Jewish temple as a marketplace to raise money.

According to Matthew, he chased all the people out of the temple who were using it as a place to do business. He announced sternly that this place was reserved for the activity of prayer, not business exchange.

This event is so isolated and so out of context; do you think it could have been a parable in action? Could this have been a staged event to bring the Pharisees' attention to him for the final aspect of his mission?

After getting some attention from this demonstration in the temple, he stayed there, and people came for healing. The children who had followed the procession as he was coming into town on the donkey were still chanting "Hosanna."

The scribes and priests inquired about the children's involvement, and Jesus gave them the message that if he could reach the children and have them believe him, then they would grow up with new beliefs (with a whole generation following him, having broken the bonds of allegiance to the old ideas) and would enter into their inner spiritual kingdom (the kingdom of heaven.

When that eventful day came to an end, Jesus went to Bethany to spend the night, and then he came back into town the following morning.

Matthew 21:23-27

When Jesus went back to Jerusalem, the priests and church leaders inquired of Jesus where he got his authority to teach his own doctrine instead of that of the scribes.

Jesus knew they were trying to get the people angry with him, so he responded in a way that could easily get the people angry with them if they did not answer carefully. He said, "If you'll answer my question first, then I will answer yours."

Matthew 21:28-32

Jesus again told the scribes and Pharisees that because they had closed minds and would not accept new ideas, even the immoral people seeking truth would discover heaven (the knowledge of God within their own minds) ahead of them. He said this is because seekers are willing to listen, consider and then change their minds when they hear a more reasonable truth, but the Pharisees were not.

Matthew 21:33-44

He told a parable relating the leaders of the church to supervisors in a vineyard. He compared the spiritual love and spiritual enthusiasm of the workers to the fruits of the vineyard. He told them that the Pharisees and scribes wanted to use the spiritual love and spiritual enthusiasm of the people to benefit themselves rather than to let the people know that this "ripe fruit" (morally developed soul, prepared for higher knowledge) is now beyond need for guidance of the priests. Jesus predicted that the opportunity to be spiritual leaders would be taken from the Jews and be given to a nation that was advising their moral people to seek direct association with God.

Matthew 22:1-14

In this parable, Jesus again alluded to the kingdom of heaven as being a place open for people to come and celebrate a wonderful event (the mystical marriage). He said that many are told of the potential for such an event and are invited to come, but they ignored the messenger as if the idea is not as important as their earthly duties. Some ignore it altogether. He sternly related the scripture-bound Jews to those who would not accept the gift: the Messiah they have been praying for, to bring their freedom. He said that God eventually stops trying to reach those who stubbornly refuse to answer the invitation (the spiritual urge) to come to the Holy Spirit (the Christ Spirit) for spiritual knowledge, while He invites others who might accept the invitation.

Jesus told them that preparation for direct communion with God is necessary first, this preparation being the cleansing of the subconscious through the development of a moral and ethical character. The development of a harmless character is merely preparation for entry into the mystical marriage. It is not the final stage of spiritual development.

Matthew 22:15-32

The trial continues as the Pharisees send in spies to trick him with questions. With feigned respect in the hope of getting him to offend the Romans they asked, "You are a fair and a wise man. So, tell us, is it lawful to pay taxes to Caesar or not?"

Jesus does not play their game or pretend to believe that they are trying to learn from him. Jesus answered, "Show me the money. Whose picture is on this coin?"

They said, "Caesar's."

"Then give to Caesar what is Caesar's and give to God those things that are God's," Jesus offered. (Jesus does not say what that is.)

The Sadducees decide to get into the game. Remember, please, that during these times in the social culture of the Israelites, a woman was the property of the man she was living with, whether father, brother, or husband. (The Pharisees believed in a resurrection of the dead at some far-off time in the end of the world. The Sadducees did not believe in the resurrection idea. Jesus catches them both in the next scene.)

The Sadducee asked, "If a man dies leaving no children and leaves his wife to his brother so she can marry him and produce children for him, then this brother dies without children and this goes on with five other brothers marrying her in their turn, then the woman dies, whose wife will she be when the dead are resurrected?

Jesus answers, "There are no marriages in the resurrection. In the resurrection, people are like angels in heaven. But let me comment on this idea of resurrection of the dead (and correct it for you). Your own Holy Book points out that to die from the body is not to be dead in spirit. In your own scriptures, it is recorded by one of your holy ancestors that God said to him, 'I am the God of Abraham, Isaac, and Jacob.' This means that He is not the God of the dead but the God of the living (and they are alive, not dead)."

Matthew 22:34-40

The Pharisees took their turn again asking in pretended reverence, as if respecting his knowledge of their Law of Moses, the Ten Commandments.

They asked, "Which is the great commandment in the law?"

Jesus answers without hesitation or evasion. (Remember that all their emphasis was on the importance of human relations and how their people should treat one another, as if there was nothing higher to consider about spirituality.)

"The first and greatest commandment is to love God with your entire being, and the second greatest is to love your neighbor as yourself." Then he added, "On these two commandments hang all the laws and the prophets (prophesies)."

Matthew 22:41-46

Jesus now asks the Pharisees a question, referring to the Psalms written by King David in ancient times and the prediction that the Messiah, teacher of the Jews, would be descendent of David. These Israelites were so locked into the worship of family that Jesus tried to break their belief system by pointing out that they were the product of God's seed and as living souls were all related equally to one another regardless of their physical blood line.

"What do you think of Christ?" (Not referring to himself at this point, but to their scriptural Christ). Jesus inquired, "Whose son is he?"

They answered, "The son of David." (They answered this because of their scriptures.)

He denies the factual interpretation of the Bible with: "If that is so, then why did David talk to Christ and call him Lord (meaning Master)? If Christ be David's Master, how is he his Son?"

They were puzzled and gave no response.

Matthew: 23

Jesus spoke to a crowd. His personal disciples were also there. He advised them to obey the rules as given by the scribes and Pharisees, not because they were right but for their safety. This is because these people had power over them to judge, condemn, and even have them killed. But, he advised, do not mistake power for righteousness. They place heavy burdens on you people but do not obey the same rules themselves. They are seeking power and adoration at your expense and are not seeking to help you with your spiritual progress. They want to be called "rabbi, rabbi" (master) and to have you serve them through fear.

"But you have only one Master; that is Christ." (Notice he does not say that he is Christ. He has said he is the Son of God, the Son of Man, and the expected liberator who was prophesied.)

"All of you are brothers. You have a common father. That is God." (Jesus does not claim to be the only son and certainly does not claim to be God.)

"Do not seek to be called master. (Seek to lead through service.) The greatest among you will be the one who is serving you, not the one who is demanding your service."

Jesus turned his attention directly to the scribes and Pharisees in the crowd and made one final effort to reach them, this time through direct chastisement and scolding.

He called them hypocrites, emphasizing the importance of integrity and the falseness of misrepresenting one's nature, causing others to make their choices based on false things they were led to believe.

He called them children of hell. (Remember that Jesus used the term children of to indicate learning from.)

If hell is the opposite of heaven, then it is also inside the soul as heaven is. It would be a place in the mind where stagnation, non-development, depression, hatred, vengeance, and sorrow reside.

He called the Pharisees blind guides (not having spiritual sight themselves and not knowing what the spiritual goal is).

"You shut up the kingdom of heaven (place of peaceful spiritual communion inside oneself) against men by making them to have their spiritual relationship with you instead of with God. You don't go into the kingdom of heaven, nor do you allow them to."

"You require them to pay tithes, but the greatest weights of the law that need to be paid are judgment (ability to discern or to choose), mercy, and faith. You strain at a gnat and swallow a camel."

"You are like a whited sepulcher filled with filth and dead man's bones." (You look clean on the outside by observance, but inside you are filled with unrighteousness.)

You (paraphrased) lament the treatment in past times of the prophets saying, "We would have listened to them and honored them and not have persecuted them." But look at yourselves and how you are treating me. You are the children (students) of those who killed the prophets, and you still are killing prophets that are sent by God."

Jesus then prophesied that teachers and prophets that he would send out to teach would also be killed by the scribes and Pharisees.

Before leaving the Temple, Jesus spoke of himself as having been alive and involved with the Israelites even before this lifetime. He said he had gathered the Hebrew nations under his guidance over and over and still the people go astray. "Now you will not see me again," he said to this crowd, "until you are ready to say blessed is he who comes in the name of the Lord."

Then he left the Temple and returned with his disciples to the Mount of Olives, a favorite place of withdrawal for Jesus.

Matthew 24

In the next segment of Matthew's story of Jesus, we see Jesus making predictions of events that would soon begin and were to last for a long period of time—wars, rumors of wars, plagues, and earthquakes.

Jesus began his predictions by pointing out the buildings of the Temple and saying that every stone with which the buildings were made would be thrown down. (He did not say God was going to do this. He merely predicted that this event would occur.) Historically, we know that later the Jews were ostracized from Jerusalem, and the city was deliberately destroyed to prevent their inhabiting it.

Matthew 24: 3

The disciples asked three questions:

- When will all this destruction take place?
- What will be the sign that you are coming? (Remember that he has said numerous times that he will return.)
- What will be the sign that the end of the world (age) is near?

He warns them that many will come in the name of (using the name) Jesus and say that they are the Christ.

He tells them to remain calm when hearing about wars elsewhere because they are just a natural result of life in these times, and their world will be secure for a little while.

This last question is answered by Jesus:

Matthew 24:7-18

"Countries will make war with one another, famines will occur, pestilence and earthquakes will happen in various places (all at the same time). This is your sign that the sorrows are beginning.

"Then, they will deliver you (the disciples) up to be afflicted and shall kill you, and ye shall be hated by all nations because of my name.

"And, many of the Israelites will turn against each other and betray one another (which they did for years after his crucifixion).

"And, false prophets will deceive many. And, because iniquity shall abound, the love of many shall wax cold. (Some who had been enthusiastic about spiritual matters would grow indifferent.) But those of you who endure until the end shall be saved."

He does not say what they will be saved from. Historically we see that those who had committed to supporting the teachings of Jesus were saved from being made outcasts from the city of Jerusalem, as the Christians were given Jerusalem after the Jews were exiled.

"After many have grown indifferent about spiritual matters, then this gospel of the kingdom shall be preached in all the world (throughout all the areas in which the Israelites were scattered) so that all have a chance to hear the gospel of the kingdom.

"Only after that will the end come."

Jesus continues preparing his personal disciples for these social and cultural changes, saying, "When you see the abomination of desolation spoken of by Daniel the prophet, (The prediction of the Messiah's crucifixion), stand in the holy place. Then let them which be in Judea flee into the mountains, let him which is on the housetop not come down to take anything out of his house, neither let him which is in the field return back to take his clothes." (This is because Jesus' converts will be hunted down, slaughtered, or fed to lions for amusement.)

Matthew 24:21

Jesus continues, "At that time there will be great tribulation such as was not since the beginning of the world to this time, nor ever shall be (again)."

Matthew 24:23-29

Still speaking directly to his disciples about current day events (not to a reader audience of the future), Jesus said: I am coming back to you after the crucifixion, but if any person says they have seen me, don't you believe it until you see me for yourself. Don't go running into every place where people report that I have been seen. I will come as light.

"Wheresoever the carcass is, there will the eagles be gathered together. (This is to say, the scavengers will try to feed on the story of my death, gaining power and glory by claiming they have seen me.) Immediately after the tribulations I have described, the sun and the moon will be darkened for a time, stars will fall, and extremely violent atmospheric conditions will arise." (According to Matthew, this did occur along with a massive earthquake on the day of his burial and a second time soon after that.)

Matthew 24:30-31

"Then my sign will appear in heaven." (He does not say what his sign is, but he has said that heaven is inside the person. So we can assume that sign would also be inside the perceiving individual and not be visible to everyone.)

"People everywhere will be in mourning, but you will see me coming in the clouds of Heaven with power and glory." (This description matches the testimony of the disciples who wrote about seeing him alive after the crucifixion; he came in a cloud of whiteness, or white light, and was glorious.)

"I will send my angels with a great sound, and my angels will gather my believers from every area of the earth." (Study the events and angels immediately following his crucifixion, beginning Matthew 27:51)

Parable of the fig tree as a metaphor for the sign

When a fig tree's branches are not yet strong and it begins to put out leaves, you know that summer is near. So likewise, you can see my branches (the people who carry his message of the kingdom within, as branches of his ministry to put out new beliefs). Then you will know the time is at the door.

Jesus said to his personal disciples, "All this will happen in your generation." Obviously, he was not speaking of the entire earth or of the end of time for the earth, but of the end of the social and geographical position of the Jewish culture, which would precede the end of the Roman Empire as the major world power.

The end of the world

Matthew 24:34
Now he began to answer their factual question about when the end of the world will occur. He said that his ideas of spiritual righteousness and the nature of God are eternal. Then in Matthew 24:36, he denies emphatically that he is God or that he knows everything that is known by God.

He said, "But the actual time of the death of the world is not known by me nor by any other living soul, only by God."

He said that he could only speak for his own mission or part in the story, and that his coming (resurrection) would be just as disbelieved as the potential for a great flood was in the days of Noah (a flood that destroyed the greatest empires of the world at that time).

You will remember that in the Noah story, Noah had told the people many times that a flood was coming (just as Jesus was now telling the Jews that they could save their culture by becoming his followers). But they did not believe him anymore than their ancestors had believed Noah about the flood.

He said that his appearance after the resurrection was not something that a person needed to sit around waiting for, but that one should prepare to greet and receive him when they did see him, just as Noah's audience had been invited and encouraged to prepare for the coming of the flood.

Again, he did not even suggest that God was going to do any of this social or geographical upheaval. He merely stated that during all these events, which to him are foreseeable cause and effect, one person working right next to another might catch a plague and die, while the person nearest them is untouched by it. He warns them with this message: Hold to the philosophy that I have given because if you should be the one taken, your belief that God loves and forgives you will assure you a position in the place that I have prepared for my followers (the paradise of the Master Jesus). If you don't hold to the philosophy and are only pretending to, then you are a hypocrite and will be afraid of God and the afterlife. If this is true for you, then you will remain a member of the hypocrites and not go into the place in paradise that I am going to prepare for those who believe my message.

He says that after all (Israelites) have had an opportunity to hear the disciples teach about the kingdom, then those who choose to adopt his philosophy of spiritual righteousness will be offered a home in the place they love, the place that he refers to as paradise. He is going away to prepare that place to receive the souls of those who adopt his philosophy of righteousness. Jesus clearly differentiates between the kingdom of heaven (which is within each person) and his kingdom in the universal realms which he calls his paradise. The kingdom of heaven is available to everyone, as it is of the Holy Spirit and inside each soul. His kingdom of paradise is available only to the spiritually righteous who have accepted him as spiritual leader for their lives. He will lead them to the kingdom of heaven if they have not already found it. He says that the spiritually righteous (as given in the Sermon on the Mount) will merit a place in his kingdom, but the unrighteous will not. Only the spiritually righteous will be permitted to live in the place he is going to prepare. (After they leave the body, they will be his students in paradise and learn about how to attain the kingdom of heaven without a need to reincarnate in the Earth.) Those who are not righteous will remain in the place of sorrow (reincarnating again and again on the earth until they discover the kingdom of heaven by some other means).

Parable of the virgins awaiting the bridegroom

Matthew 25:1
Other parables follow, each indicating the importance of taking personal responsibility for one's own choices and preparation for spiritual awakening. No one can give that preparation to another. Each must do it for

himself or herself. First must come the purification by actualizing morality in the consciousness; then one is ready for the greater understanding to come.

Jesus prepares for his final demonstration.

Matthew 26

Jesus told his disciples that the feast of the Passover was in two days, and that afterwards he would be arrested and crucified. In this segment of his ministry, we see him denying that the purpose for living is to try to make a paradise of this world.

Matthew 26: 10-12:

He said that poverty will always be in the world and that to show love by causing pleasure is just as righteous as to show love by eliminating suffering.

Jesus spent some time in the house of Simon of Bethany where a woman came and anointed his head with very expensive oil while he ate. Matthew reports that all the disciples protested and were indignant that the woman would waste this valuable oil for the pleasure of one man instead of using it for charity. Jesus said that her intent and her action were good (caring, nurturing, loving) and that no amount of charity would ever eliminate the poverty from the earth. "The poor will be with you always."

Judas Deals with the Chief Priest of the Jews

On the first feast day, Jesus sent his disciples to a specific man and told them to say that Jesus had sent a message. The message was, "My time is at hand. I will keep the Passover at your house with my disciples." (Obviously he had collaborators.)

Once they were in that man's home, in an upper room, as they ate their Passover meal (a Jewish religious ritual), Jesus said that one of them would betray him. He identified Judas as the one, as if it were an assignment.

Judas inquired, "Is it I?"

Jesus confirmed, "You have said so."

Judas left to go and do as he was selected to do. While Jesus and the others ate, Jesus spoke with poetic sadness of the event that was rapidly approaching.

I break this bread like my body will be broken.

I pour out this wine like my blood will be poured out.(Spilled so that many could understand and be free from their burdensome belief that God is punishing them)

But these things are necessary *so that even more people can believe* that the Messiah has come and that now they are free from paying for the sins of Adam and Eve and all their other ancestors. "Everyone of you will abandon me tonight, but when I return, I will lead you into Galilee."

Peter denied that he would abandon Jesus. But Jesus knew that Peter was not as solid or steady as a rock. He predicted, "Before the cock crows tomorrow morning, you will have denied me three times." Peter vowed that he would stay close by and that he would even die with Jesus in order to protect him.

Jesus Prays in the Garden of Gethsemane

Once they were in the garden, Jesus made a request of his disciples, "Wait here while I go and pray."

He took Peter and the two sons of Zebedee with him closer to his place of prayer. There he shared his feelings with them, admitting that he was in grief. He said, "My soul is sorrowful. Sit here and watch (for the arresting officers) while I go and pray."

Jesus again demonstrated that he was not claiming to be *God,* but that he was relating to God as a confidante. Being true to the spirit of his mission, he prayed, presenting his preference of the outcome, while stating that he would accept whatever outcome arose as Divine Order for his mission. His stated preference was that people change their minds, making it unnecessary for him to endure the arrest and crucifixion in order to have them understand that life is in the soul.

He found his three friends asleep and voiced his disappointment. Then he sternly asked the same disciples again to watch while he prayed. The same prayer or preference was voiced, along with his commitment to fulfill the scriptural prophesies, if he must, in order to influence more to believe that he was their expected spiritual teacher.

He came out of prayer to find the three disciples sleeping again and not guarding him.

He returned to his place of prayer to make the same supplication a third time.

After that prayer, he knew that no amount of praying on his part was going to change their minds. Some would change their minds when the script had been played out. Others would not change. He psychically perceived that Judas and the guards were approaching and knew that he was now entering into the final stage of the script as given in the Jewish scriptures.

Jesus confirms that God is not requiring this of him. He has volunteered.

When one of the disciples took out a sword to resist and cut off the ear of a soldier, Jesus stopped him and reminded him of the law of cause and effect. He also reminded the disciple that he was not without the power to stop this himself if he chose not to go through with it. He could assert his personal will and pray to God for helpers, he said, and then 12 legions of angels would come to save him. But "how then shall their *scriptures be fulfilled?*" This was vital in order to convince some of his followers.

Jesus was subjected to accusations and questioning by the high priest of the Jews, but he remained silent, offering no explanation or defense. He was then turned over to the Roman authorities with a demand that he be found guilty and crucified. The Roman judge said, "I find no fault with him."

After many efforts to give the case back to the Jewish courts and eventually appealing to Jesus to speak up in his own behalf, the Roman judge accepted the duty of responsibility of his position as a Roman judge. (Jesus knew that if he spoke up with the truth, he would be released since no crime had been committed. He was not willing to lie or to admit to something he had not done. Therefore, he remained silent in order to not interfere with the outcome.)

As Jesus was being tried, Peter was standing near the palace. He was recognized by some of the people who inquired, "Aren't you one of his disciples?"

Three times he was asked if he knew Jesus. Three times he said "no." When the cock crowed as dawn broke, Peter remembered what Jesus had said, and he felt ashamed.

The Interrogation and Crucifixion
According to Matthew

Jesus was asked, "Are you the Christ?" He did not answer. (His refusal to be involved assures that he will have no influence over the outcome as he has decided to let the script play out as Divine Order unfolded)

He was asked, "Are you the King of the Jews?" He answered, "Thou sayest." (That is what you say.)

He was crucified and mocked.

His final words are reported to be, "My God, my God, why hast thou forsaken me?" This is a quote from the old Jewish scriptures, yet another effort to point out to them that he was the fulfillment of their expectation for liberation of the Jews from their tyrannical religious control. He was quoting Psalms 22:1, written by David, the second King of the Israelites, hundreds of years before the birth of Jesus.

Matthew wrote that an earthquake occurred immediately following Jesus' final breath, damaging the Temple, and opening grave sites. Taking the coincidence of the darkness and the earthquake at his death as signs, a centurion said, "Surely this was the Son of God." (Another indication of people looking to the scriptures to prove something to them.)

Because it was a Jewish holiday and routine burials were not done on their holidays, the body was placed temporarily in the burial tomb of a wealthy sympathizer with intent to move his body after the holiday was over.

Matthew wrote that a woman who sat by his tomb saw an angel who told her Jesus was going into Galilee to meet his disciples. (I will send my angels.) And Jesus met them saying "Be not afraid. Go and tell my brothers to meet me in Galilee." (I will go before thee into Galilee.)

CHAPTER SIX

Gospel Writers Differ About the End of the Story

Matthew

Being one of the 11 remaining disciples and personally present at this occurrence, Matthew reports that the disciples had been expecting this and they went right away to Galilee. He wrote that Jesus had selected this place before the crucifixion as the place of their rendezvous upon his return. There he spoke to them saying, "Go ye and teach all nations. Teach them to observe all things I have given you, and lo, I am with you always even unto the end of the world."

Mark

In reading the book of Mark, we see that Mark, who was not one of the disciples and who did not know Jesus personally, reports the end of the story very differently. He says that the disciples were surprised and frightened to see Jesus (Mark:16). This seems very out of character when, according to Matthew who was a disciple, the disciples knew all along what Jesus was planning to do.

Luke

Luke, who also was not one of the disciples and who did not know Jesus personally, was a friend of Mark and follower of Paul. He wrote that Jesus came to the disciples in Jerusalem unexpectedly and that they were frightened of him. This disagrees with what the disciples, John, and Matthew, reported about their response.

John

The other writer, who was a personal friend and disciple of Jesus just as Matthew was, reports the opposite of Luke or Mark. He wrote that Jesus came to the disciples in a room in Jerusalem where they were hiding from the Jews. He says that they were happy to see him. John tells of a second visit from Jesus to a few of the disciples while they were in a ship.

Two points to keep in mind:

- After Jesus' mission was over, the Jews were indeed cast out of Jerusalem (the end of their world).

- Later, Jesus' followers became the inhabitants of Jerusalem (given that city by the Romans).

CHAPTER SEVEN

Excerpts from the Book of John

Just as any skilled writer, John sets up his premises before beginning his story of Jesus. John truly believes that Jesus is God, and he states that in the outset of his story. Then he attempts to prove it with the episodes that he reports.

John 1:38-39

The action and words of Jesus, as given by John, begin with the scene of Jesus walking close to a place where John the Baptist (not this writer, John) is teaching. Two men follow Jesus, and Jesus turns to ask them what they want.

They answer by addressing him as "Rabbi" and asking where he lives.

He invites them to follow him home.

They follow and stay the entire day with him in his home.

This is the beginning of John's rendition of how and in what order Jesus selected his personal disciples. Take time to compare this to Matthew's memory of how it occurred.

The story of Jesus turning the water to wine is given next. Notice that this is not a part of Jesus' teaching. It is a story told by the writers. The important point here is that Jesus obviously had been doing some amazing miracles with his mother as witness. He responded to her that it was not yet time for him to begin his ministry. Nevertheless, he indulged her. This story has no bearing on the study of his message.

Early in Jesus' ministry, almost in the very beginning of it, is where John places the story of Jesus driving the animals and the money changers out of the temple.

Remember that Matthew placed this story at the end of Jesus' ministry, at a point when he could afford to cause some anger and outrage on the part of the priests.

John 2:19

John reports that Jesus went about the whole territory doing miracles and announcing to the priests that he was the Christ. He says that after having been asked by the Jews what sign he will give to prove his identity as the Messiah (John uses the word Christ).

John 3: 3-8

In John's book, Jesus' actual teaching begins with a private conversation between Jesus and a man named Nicodemus who came to him secretly. Nicodemus wanted to know how he could see the kingdom of God.

Jesus answered, unless a person be born again, he can't see the kingdom of God. Then he explained: The first birth is of water; this is the birth into the world. The second birth is of spirit; this is the birth into the kingdom of God. Unless you are born of the second birth, the birth of spirit, you cannot enter into the experience of the kingdom of God. You cannot decide when it will happen to you. It comes when the necessary conditions are present in one's consciousness.

Spiritual birth is an event that comes and then is gone, just as any birth is an event, not an ongoing experience. One's development before birth is of one kind, and development after birth is of another kind. The development before spiritual birth is of one kind—moral and socialization development. The development after spiritual birth is of another kind. Spiritual birth is the dawning of one's realization of an inner sense of harmony, beauty, goodness, and perfection that is not related to people, nature, or anything else in the outer world. It is the experience of the Holy Spirit within one's own soul. After the spiritual birth, the development of the soul is an increase of the sensing of this Substance until the very Source of the Substance is encountered, transcendent to self.

Nicodemus still does not understand. He tries to relate, but he is imagining a physical birth in some other place called spirit.

"What? You are an Israelite Master, and you can't understand these things?" Jesus responds.

He predicts his crucifixion and the inevitability of it
John 3:14

"In the same way that Moses lifted the serpent in the wilderness, I must be lifted up so that those who believe I am the Christ will be free" (from ignorance of God). (In the Jewish book of Numbers, Moses makes a serpent of brass, puts it on a pole and raises it up.)

John 3:16-18

"For God so loved the world that he gave his only begotten son." If God is Spirit, as Jesus said, then the Son of God must also be Spirit. One is the source of the seed, and the other is the developed seed. One is the Original Divine Essence (God), and the other is the Secondary Divine Essence (the Christ Spirit in each of us). The Christ Spirit, Son of God, is developed from a seed projected out of God-Mind and placed in the soul of each of us.

"God gave his only begotten son so that whosoever believes in him (in God) will have everlasting life. (You will recall that life has been defined as knowledge of God. Thus, Jesus is saying, "God gave the Christ

Spirit to humanity so that whoever believes in God will have everlasting knowledge of God." Simply stated, your inner Christ will give you the knowledge of God that you need for your spiritual birth and further development. It is up to you to use that knowledge for your spiritual development.

"God sent not his son(s) into the world to condemn the world but that the world through him might be saved" (from not knowing God).

God did not provide the Christ Spirit in you to condemn you, but to save you from death. Since death is the opposite of life, this would mean to save you from being without knowledge of God.

"He that believes on him (on God) is not condemned, but he that believes not is already condemned because he has not believed in the name of the Son of God." A name is a symbol for a thing or an idea. One must believe that there is a Spirit within that will provide knowledge of God, or else be condemned to ignorance of God, as that is the only way to gain that subjective knowledge. For those who have not found the inner Christ, Jesus is a symbol or example of the Christ Spirit in expression until they find their own inner Christ Spirit to serve as their guide.

Jesus defines the condemnation that disbelief will produce

John 3:19-21

"This is the condemnation: that light is come into the world and men loved darkness (not seeing the truth) rather than light (seeing the truth) because their deeds were evil" (and they did not want to see that). Therefore, the condemnation he speaks of is not a punishment but a self-imposed condemnation to ignorance of the power of the inner Christ to give one personal knowledge of God that expands as one grows in Spirit.

Simply phrased: If a person chooses to remain unknowing when greater knowledge is offered, then by his/her choice the result is to remain unknowing.

"Everyone who does evil hates to perceive the truth of the matter and avoids coming into spiritual knowledge in order to avoid feeling guilty. But one who does truth (not falseness or deceit) comes willingly into the light" (not afraid of God or self or others perceiving what he has been doing. In fact, he wants to be aware of what he has been doing in order to correct his own errors and faulty habits.)

John 4:1-5

John says that Jesus then went around teaching and baptizing until he heard that the Pharisees were unhappy with him for taking such authority on himself, and he decided to leave Judea and go back to Galilee. In order to get there, he had to go through Samaria, a village that had been given to Joseph by his father, Jacob, and was still inhabited by the descendants of Joseph.

Jesus sat down on a well waiting for his disciples to return from shopping for food. He was thirsty but had nothing to draw the water with. A woman came to the well and let down her bucket, and he asked for some water.

She was very surprised that he would speak to her, a Samaritan. The Jewish tribes believed themselves to be chosen by God. The Samaritans were descendants of tribes that were outcast. Outcast Israeli tribes were not spoken to by the Jewish tribes.

"If you knew who I am, you would ask me for a drink, and I would give you living water," Jesus responded. (I would quench your spiritual thirst with knowledge of God.)

"Sir, where would you get this water?"

Jesus answered, "Whoever drinks of this water will never thirst again. The water will stay in him like a well of water springing up into everlasting life." (Everlasting knowledge of God).

"Sir, give me this water so that I never have to come to this well again."

Jesus said, "Go and get your husband."

"I have no husband," the woman said.

"You have told the truth," said Jesus. "You have had four husbands, and the man you are now living with is not your husband."

Then the woman spoke with amazement. "You must be a prophet (a psychic). Our fathers (Joseph and his descendants) worshiped in this mountain, but your people, the Jews, say that everyone is required to worship in Jerusalem."

"There is a time coming soon when people will not be concerned about which land area they are supposed to be worshiping in. True worshipers everywhere will worship in spirit and in truth, not a specified city or temple. God is a Spirit. And those who worship God must worship him in spirit and in truth, Jesus said.

The woman discounted the possibility that Jesus knew the truth. "Well, the Messiah is coming someday. When he comes, he will tell us everything."

Jesus said, "I that speak unto thee am he."

She ran to tell her people that the Messiah was among them.

In the meantime, the disciples returned with food. Jesus was feeling pretty successful and fulfilled in his encounter with the woman and the fact that she believed him.

"Eat," they said, offering him food.

"I have food to eat that you do not know of," Jesus replied.

"Did someone give you food while we were gone?" they asked.

"No. My food is to do the will of God and to do his work. You say that there are four months to harvest time, but I say the harvest is ready now." His harvest is the people that are ready to change their beliefs; their harvest is of earthly produce.)

Jesus said (to paraphrase), "Those who came before us (spiritual leaders before us) have sown seeds, and now the fruit is ripe and ready. We will reap. Those who plant (seeds) and those who reap will rejoice together. I'll send you to reap that upon which you bestowed no labor, so you are now involved in the work of the laborers."

He stayed two more days with the Samaritans, talking to them about the kingdom of heaven, and many believed everything that he said. Then he went on to Galilee.

In Galilee they were not asking about the kingdom but remembered his miracles and were asking for more free miracles. He did some healing work, as they were not receptive to his message of the kingdom. Then he went back to Jerusalem to continue his work of attracting crowds and delivering his message.

John 5:6-14

Jesus challenged a man who desired healing to make some effort in helping himself rather than think other people were supposed to do everything for him. Then Jesus did part of the healing and said, "Your part is to go and wash, then separate yourself from God no more (sin no more) lest a worse thing come to you."

Some people believe that Jesus said God will bring something worse to the man, but he did not say that. He merely imparted knowledge of the law of cause and effect to this man, letting him know that doing things that are not in harmony with spiritual good will bring results that are not in harmony with spiritual good. To be healed does not mean that one will remain well. For those who wish to remain healthy, there are certain things to be considered.

The Jews protest that he healed on the Sabbath

The Jews got angry and wanted to kill him because he was healing on the Sabbath. Jesus said to them, "My Father works on the Sabbath, and I work on the Sabbath."

John 5:18-21

Jews want to kill him because he said God is his father.

Jesus said, "I cannot do anything except what I have perceived that God does. For whatever I perceive of as God's work, I do the same (as an agent of God). Because God loves me and shows me all the things that He does, I know He will show me even greater works than these (as I inquire and observe). And as God raises up the dead (ignorant) and gives life (knowledge of God) to them, so will I."

God Does Not Judge

John 5:22-47

Jesus said, "And God judges NO MAN; but God has given all (power) of judgment to the Son (the one knowing the Holy Spirit has judgment) so that men should honor the Son as they honor the Father. If you dishonor me, you are also dishonoring God because He sent me. And here is the truth: Anyone of you who hears my words and believes on Him (God) has everlasting life (knowledge of God) and shall not come into judgment but is passed directly from death (ignorance) to life (knowledge of God).

"Soon the dead (those without true knowledge of God) will hear my voice, and they that hear will live (have knowledge of God). God has life (self-knowledge) in Himself, and He has put life (knowledge of

Himself) in me and has given me authority to exercise judgment because I am of Him (just as everyone who attains the awakening of the inner Christ has authority to exercise spiritual judgment for themselves)."

Remember his reference to the spiritual birth when he spoke to Nicodemus (John 3:3-8).

"Soon all who are in the graves shall hear God's voice and come forth into the renewal of life (renewal of spiritual knowledge). Those who have done good will come forth to the resurrection of life; and those who have done evil will come forth into the renewal of their anguish. I can of myself do nothing (about all this). Even as I hear, I judge (discern), and the conclusions are fair because I judge by the will of God (as a standard) and not by my own will… John (the Baptist) told you about me. And I tell you about God. I don't tell you what others have told me about God. I tell you what I have seen.

Yes, John told you about me, and now I demonstrate by my work (actions) that I am the Messiah as John says that I am. You search the scriptures to try to find eternal life, and your scriptures describe me. They say that I will come to teach you. Yet you will not come to me (you prefer the book over the messenger that the book predicted). If you had the love of God in you, you would recognize the truth when you hear it. I come saying I am sent by God, and because of that you reject me (inferring, didn't your scriptures tell you that I would say that?). If I came saying I am coming of my own accord (instead of that I am on a mission from God), you would accept me. Your block to believing is that you honor the writers of books more than you honor God. Don't be afraid that I will accuse you to

God. It is not I, but Moses who accuses you (says you are guilty)."

Notice how the term believed in means to believe that person told the truth.

"If you had (really) believed in Moses, you would have believed in me (because he said I would come). But if you don't believe in Moses (what Moses said in predicting me), then my demonstration will have no meaning to you."

The story of the five loaves and two fishes

John 6:4-14

John places this story at a different timeframe in Jesus' ministry than Matthew did. Matthew says that these are the people who followed Jesus and lay the palm branches when he was returning to

Jerusalem, just before the crucifixion. But the story of the event, itself, is basically the same, even to the number of men who were there.

John 6:26-29

John reports that as they followed him, Jesus said to them, "You have not followed me because of the miracle, but because your hunger was fed. Now, work for that food that will prevent your hunger from ever returning" (feed your spiritual hunger by listening to my message).

"How can we work the works of God like you do?" they wanted to know. (They are speaking of the miracles.)

But Jesus explains that to do the work of God is to believe the truth that he is giving. "This is the work of God: That you would believe me." (Thus, he has explained what he meant when he said to work for that food that will prevent hunger.) He meant believe me so that your hunger for God will be fed, and you will never suffer from that hunger again.

John 6:30

"Our fathers (ancestors) ate manna in the desert. God gave them bread directly from Heaven," the people said. (They are inferring that they want to see that miracle repeated. Exodus 16 tells the story of manna from heaven.)

Jesus said, "I am the bread that God has sent to you. My words are spiritual food that fills the soul with spiritual truth. I came down from God (this was his major sacrifice) to do God's will and not my own.

"And this is God's will: That all of you (his audience is the Jews) who see me and believe I am the one sent to you by Him may have everlasting life" (everlasting knowledge of God, knowledge that you will never forget).

The Jews murmured.

John 6:41-51

Jesus said (in paraphrase), "Never mind. If you are not drawn to me, it is because you are not yet ready (ripe for the spiritual harvest). It is because God is not drawing you to me. Spirit draws my people to me. Only those which are of God have seen the Father, and (because they have seen God) they recognize me. (They know I am doing spiritual things and saying spiritual truth.) He that believes that I am the promised one has everlasting life (knowledge of God). He will feed on me (consume my spiritual food). Yes, your fathers ate manna from Heaven, but they are dead. If you consume the bread (spiritual food/words of truth) that I offer, you will not die" (not remain ignorant of God as they were).

Jesus explains eating his flesh and drinking his blood

John 6:61

"If I give up the flesh and give up the blood (and don't try to keep it from you), I still have my Spirit. That is my life. It is Spirit that gives the life, not flesh and blood." (paraphrased)

"The words I speak are spirit. They are life (knowledge of God). But some of you don't believe me. As I said, God draws my own to me."

The crowd left, and Jesus said to his twelve personal disciples, "Will you also walk away?"

Simon Peter protests and vows his acceptance. Jesus says, "I have chosen you twelve, but one of you is a devil." (He has previously called Peter, Satan, so we know he uses this word very facetiously.)

Jesus then went to teach in Galilee, and still the people there were mainly interested in his miracles. They urged him to go back into Jerusalem to teach because they thought he was a fake. He said, "My time has not yet come."

He knew that the next time he entered Jerusalem, he would be arrested.

John 7:10-39
Very soon afterwards he went anonymously to join in the festive celebrations in

Jerusalem, and then he taught openly in the Temple.

"Moses gave you the law: Thou shalt not kill. Yet you seek to kill me…You circumcise a boy on the Sabbath to keep the law of Moses from being broken. But when I make a man whole on the Sabbath, you want to kill me…God has sent me… and in a little while, I will go to Him who sent me. You will seek me and shall not find me, and where I am going you cannot come."

The Jews asked, "Where will he go? Will he go to teach the Gentiles?"

On the day of feasting, Jesus is in the Temple teaching.

"If you are thirsty, come unto me and drink. Then out of your belly will flow living waters." (John comments that they did not know he was speaking of spirit when he said water. John specifically identifies his belief that the water Jesus meant was the Holy Spirit.)

John 8:1-11

Jesus went to the Mount of Olives to rest and then back to the temple to teach.

Many people came to hear him. The Pharisees brought an adulterous woman before him to try to make him judge her (trying to make a liar of him because he had said, "God does not judge, but has power to do so, which He gave to me, and I do not judge.")

The Pharisees said, "Moses' law says to stone her."

They believed he would have to either break the law of Moses, a criminal offense, or make a judgment against a person, as he said he would not do. Jesus took some time to think. Then he said, "Whoever is without sin, cast the first stone at her."

Everyone left.

"I do not condemn," Jesus said to her. "Go your way. (Then he said to her what he had said to the blind man, not with any malice or threat, but as a warning, to pay attention to the law of cause and effect.) "Go your way and sin (separate yourself from God) no more."

The Pharisees and others return

John 8:12-23

Jesus resumes his teaching.

"I am the light" (the one who will help you perceive the truth). "If you follow me, you will not walk in darkness (ignorance), but in light (perceiving).

Pharisees call him on it, as boasting is considered a lie in their culture

They said, "You are witnessing for yourself, so it is not true."

Jesus said, "l know where l have been and where l am going. You do not… You judge after the flesh (what you see with your physical eyes). I judge no man."

"Where is your Father?" the Pharisees demanded.

"You don't know me or my Father, Jesus said, "If you had known one, you would have recognized the other… I'm going away. You'll seek me (in the scriptures), but you will die (remain ignorant) in your sins (sense of separateness from God). You cannot go where I am going."

"Does he plan to kill himself?" they wondered.

Jesus continued to speak. "You are from beneath; I am from above. You are of this world; I am not of this world."

John 8:24-28

"If you hold onto your belief that the Messiah has not come, you will die in your belief that God punishes for sins."

"Who are you?" the Pharisees continued to probe.

"The same as I said in the beginning. You will know that I am the one you have been waiting for when you lift me up (on the cross) and you will know that I have no power of my own" (to do the things I have been doing).

John 8:29-32

"But as God has taught me, I speak. You will know that God is with me."

Some believed him.

Jesus says those who continue in believing his words, are his students. The truth shall make you free from bondage to a belief that God punishes.

John 8

Jesus asks why they don't you understand his speech? Is it because they are not hearing?

Jesus tries again to reach their minds

Jesus tried to explain his relationship to God as one who is directly guided by God as they have been guided by a man—Abraham. And you obey his word from old scriptures and call him your father. Ultimately, he says that if they know God they will perceive that he is telling the truth and if they do not know God, they will not believe him

John 8:48-59

The Jews said he was a Samaritan and that he had a devil in him.

Jesus argued that he had no devil and sought no glory for himself. He said that if a person would keep his teachings, they would never see death.

Jews pointed out that Abraham and all the prophets were already dead, yet Jesus was saying that those who believe him will never die. To them this meant he was saying he was greater than Abraham and the dead prophets, and they asked him who he was trying to make himself out to be.

Jesus said he would not lie in order to keep out of trouble and that to say he does not know God would be a lie. He said that God honored him by giving him words to say and that Abraham was happy to see his day come.

The Jews are having a good time making fun of Jesus for saying he had seen Abraham.

Then Jesus said that he preceded Abraham.

They took up stones to throw at him

John 9

The story of Jesus healing the blind man is symbolic of Jesus' mission of helping people have a clearer perception that God does not punish. (They even believed that death was a punishment for sins.)

John 9:5

Jesus says that he is in the world to help people see the truth.

John 9:22

The Jews had agreed that if anyone should suggest that Jesus was Christ, he should be put out of the synagogue, excommunicated.

Jesus speaks to Pharisees about his mission

John 10:7-11

Jesus says that he is the doorway to spiritual understanding). If any man accepts what he says, that one will be saved (from his false beliefs about God). He had identified life as knowledge of God.

He is the shepherd, leading people into new beliefs.

John 10:30-42

When he said that he was one with God in spirit, they took up stones to stone him.

Jesus asked why they wanted to stone him, noting that he did only good and that God was in him and he was in God.

He escaped as they tried to stone him, going into the wilderness beyond Jordan. Many followed him and said they believed him.

Jesus demonstrates that life is in the soul.

John 11

Jesus was sent for when his personal friend, Lazarus, was very ill. He deliberately waited until Lazarus had died to go to the home of the family. When Jesus arrived, the man had been dead for four days. Many Jews from Jerusalem had come to comfort the sisters.

Jesus acknowledged that Lazarus was dead. He said that he was glad that it happened when he was not there because he wanted them to see that life is not of the body but in the soul. He said Lazarus would rise again.

A sister said she knew he would rise again at the resurrection time.

The Israelites' belief was that a time of resurrection would come at the end of the world. Until that time, all dead people were unconscious in their graves. When that day came, God would raise the bones of all dead people and give them flesh again. God would then judge them one at a time to determine whether they would be thrown off the earth into outer darkness of space or whether they would stay on Earth, at which point would be the restored Eden.

Jesus states that he *is* the resurrection and that anyone who believes what he teaches, even though they have died will live.

Jesus felt compassion for the grief of those who cared for Lazarus. He wept for their pain, but they thought he was weeping because Lazarus was dead. Jesus prayed aloud for Lazarus soul to return to the body to demonstrate that life is in the soul and that the dead are not sleeping and unconscious in their graves. Lazarus' soul returned to his body, and he came walking out of the tomb. Some of the Jews stayed behind. Others rushed to tell the chief priests and Pharisees what had happened.

John reports that now the Pharisees were afraid that because of Jesus' great power, the Romans would come and kill them all. The chief priest reasoned with the other Pharisees that it was better for one man (Jesus) to die in order to save them from the

Romans, than for all Jews to be killed by them. He said that Jesus' death would save the whole nation from the Roman's slaughter. For that he would be a hero for having saved not only Jerusalem but all the Israelites.

From that day on, the Jews held meetings to decide how they might put him to death. Jesus knew about this plot and did not walk openly among them anymore.

The Pharisees had given a commandment in the Temple that if any man knew where Jesus was, he must tell so they might take him and save the nation from the Roman's slaughter.

John 12:9-19

Many spectators went to see Lazarus for themselves and believed that Jesus was the expected Messiah.

On the feast day of the Passover, large numbers of them, hearing that he was coming, spread branches of palm trees as a carpet for Jesus to ride upon. They sang out that he was the King of Israel, as David and Solomon had been, who had come in the name of the Lord.

Jesus found a donkey and rode upon it into the city because that was what the scriptures had said he would do. (The script called for it.) The Pharisees talked among themselves saying they have made no progress in their plan, because so many Jews are still following him.

John 12:23-27
Jesus announced that his time to be killed has come and that he is troubled, yet he knew this was the purpose for his being in this situation.

Even though he had told them many times, the disciples did not believe that he was going to be killed.

John glosses over the final supper that Matthew carefully described and reports what Jesus did after the meal.

John 13:4-17

After the meal, Jesus washed the feet of his disciples. Peter refused to allow it, but Jesus indicated it was a symbol of purification and partnership with him.

Then Jesus explained that he was setting an example that he would like them to follow. He asked that his disciples act as partners and helpers to one another. He said that all people are equal, even though one might be a master, or a teacher to the others, because the master teacher is a servant to those he teaches. (serving knowledge)

Jesus identifies Judas as the one to betray him and sends him to perform the task

John 13:18-30

Jesus says that he knows who he has chosen as partners and that, in order to fulfill the ancient Jewish scriptures, he deliberately chose one whom he knew would betray him.

John asked which one it would be.

Jesus answered that it would be the one to whom he offered a "sop" after he had dipped it. He then dipped it and gave it to Judas, telling him to do it quickly.

Judas went immediately to turn him in.

Jesus' Farewell Statements to Disciples

John 14:2-6

"In my Father's house are many mansions; if it were not so, I would have told you. I go to prepare a place for you. After I prepare that place, I will come to you again and receive you so that you can know the place is ready for you. You know where I am going, and you know the way."

Thomas said, "But we do not know where you are going. How can we know the way?"

Jesus answered that the way he had taught them was the only way that anyone could go to the Father. (through the Holy Spirit)

John 13:34
Jesus told his disciples to regard each other with love. Surely he knew that there would

be much controversy among them as they tried to determine what he wanted them to teach after he was gone. He would have known that an order to regard each other with love would help considerably to limit competitiveness and arguments among themselves.

John 14:9-20

Having previously said that God is a Spirit, Jesus emphasizes this, saying that he is in that Spirit and that Spirit is in him. He says that he has been acting in response to that Spirit of God all along and that his activities in his ministry were expressions of that Spirit of God which he had learned from God.

"He that believes on me (believes what I have said), shall do the works I have done and even greater works." (He does not suggest that there is no development required before one can do those works.)

"If you ask anything in my name, I will do it. (He does not say how long the response time

might be.) "I will pray to the Father that He give you a comforter to live with you forever. That comforter is the Spirit that will teach you the truth… In a little while, the Jews will see me no

more, but you will see me because I live. You also shall live. Because I live (have knowledge of God) you will live (have knowledge of God), also. When you see me again, you will know that God and you and I all are in the same Spirit."

I will manifest to those who love me, keep my commandments.

John 14:21

A disciple inquires, "How is it that you can manifest yourself to us and not to the world?" Jesus explains that the Spirit in him empowers him to communicate personally with anyone who loves him and also honors his message.

Jesus continues this very private conversation with his personal disciples.

John 14:27 through 15:7

"Do not be troubled… If you loved me, you would be happy that I am going to the Father for my Father is greater than I. I am like a vine, but the Father is the owner of the vineyard. The people who are attached to me are like branches of me. Those branches will not remain attached to me if they do not produce that which can be used as spiritual food for others. But those who do produce fruit will be cleansed so they can produce even more spiritual food. You, my disciples, are now cleansed and are committed to passing on the spiritual food that I have inspired in you. If you don't stay in communion with me, no one will find spiritual food as a result of your efforts. But if you do stay in communion with me, my words will stay alive in you, and you will produce much spiritual food for others to feed upon."

John 15:8

"So ye shall be my disciples" (my students).

This was said at the close of Jesus' ministry. Therefore, to continue to be his students would be to continue to be taught by him.

John 15:15

"I do not think of you as my servants, for a servant does not know what his master is doing. But I call you my friends because I have shared with you the communication I have received from God. I have chosen you and I have ordained you so that you can go and produce spiritual food and that the spiritual food you offer will remain."

Several times during this final communication with his personal friends, Jesus said, "My commandment is that you love (express loving regard) one another."

"And don't be concerned if the world (their world is the Jewish/Roman society) hates you. They hated me, too. If you were one of them, it would love its own. But I have chosen you out of that society, so now they hate you. Those who are persecuting me will also persecute you. (You are not exempt from the world's persecution just because they persecuted me first.) Those who accepted me will accept you. They do not know God, so they will judge you by how they feel about me. If I had not come to give them the truth, they would still have a lie to hide behind when they practice acts of spiritual ignorance . . . but now they can no longer pretend they do not know how to gain knowledge of God. I have told them how, and they hated what I told them… I tell you all this so that you will not be surprised or offended when they put you out of the synagogues. They will believe that by killing you, they are doing it for God… When your persecution comes, you will remember what I told you and be comforted by the knowledge that I spoke the truth… So, now I am going to him that sent me, and not one of you has asked me where I am going! You're too busy being sorrowful… I have to go away so that you will depend on the Holy Spirit in yourselves and not on me. As long as I am here, you will be looking to me for learning of God. The Holy Spirit will give you true knowledge of how to practice spiritual judgment for your own lives."

John 16:19-33

His friends ask what he means about being seen, then not being seen, and being seen again. He explains that they will weep for him, but that his pain and theirs will be transient, because he will see them again, and they will rejoice. "And your joy no man taketh away. I am speaking to you (not directly) but in proverb. But soon I will be more plain about what I am telling you. I came to earth from God, and I will leave the world and go to God. In the world, you will have tribulation, but in thinking of me, you will find peace."

John 17:3-17

Jesus said that to know God is life eternal.

Jesus speaks to God:

"And this is life eternal: that they might know thee, the only true God, and Jesus Christ whom thou hast sent. I have finished the work that you gave me to do. I have known you since before the world was. I have convinced the men that you sent me to reach. Now I ask that you show the world that I was sent by you. (Glorify me.)"

I am not praying for all the Jewish society, but specifically for my personal disciples and all those who will believe them… I ask that you sanctify them (keep them from being dissuaded by the treatment they will receive).

The Interrogation and Crucifixion

John 18:13

John reports that Jesus was first taken to the Jewish high priest, the one who had given the idea that it was expedient that one man should die in lieu of all the people.

John 18:19 through 19:42

When asked by the high priest what the doctrine was that he preached, Jesus answered that he had never taught secretly but openly in the synagogue and in the temple. "So why do you ask what I have taught? Why not ask those who heard me."

Jesus was then to be taken to the judgment hall to be sentenced by the Romans. Pilate went out of the hall to speak to them. "What is he accused of?"

They answered indignantly that if he were not a malefactor, they would not have brought him to the judgment hall.

"Then you take him and judge him according to your law," said Pilate.

The Jews responded, "It is not lawful for us to put any man to death." (They were letting Pilate know they wanted Jesus to be lawfully put to death.)

Pilate went back into the judgment hall and called to Jesus, "Are you the King of the Jews?"

"Are you asking this for yourself, or did others tell it to you about me?" Jesus asked.

Pilate said, "Am I a Jew? Your own people have brought you to me. What have you done?"

"My Kingdom is not of this world," said Jesus.

Pilate inquired, "Are you a king, then?"

"You say that I am a king," said Jesus. "To this end (the crucifixion) was I born, and the reason I came into the world was to bear witness to the truth. Everyone that is of the truth hears my voice."

"What is truth?" raged Pilate in frustration.

Then he went directly back out to the Jews. "I find no fault in him at all. But you have a Passover custom that I release to you one of your people who is sentenced to death. Shall I release him to you?"

They all cried out together, "No, release Barabbas" (a robber who was scheduled for crucifixion that day).

Then Pilate took Jesus and had him scourged. The soldiers made him a crown of thorns to make fun of the title he was accused of claiming, King of the Jews. They put a purple robe on him (to further make fun of him with the color of royalty).

Pilate went out again to appeal to the people. "I bring him forth to you again, to tell you that I find no fault in him." And Jesus came forth wearing the crown of thorns and purple robe.

Then the chief priests and officers began to cry out, "Crucify him."

"You take him and crucify him," said Pilate. "I find no fault in him."

"We have a law," warned the Jews, "and by our laws he ought to die because he said he is the

Son of God."

When Pilate heard this, he was even more reluctant to pronounce the sentence. He went to Jesus and asked, "Where did you come from?"

Jesus did not respond.

Pilate appealed to Jesus to defend himself and to cooperate by simply answering the questions. "Don't you know I have the power to release you? I can judge either way."

"The only power you have is the power God has given you. Those who brought me to you have the greater fault," answered Jesus.

After that Pilate sought to release him, but the Jews threatened to accuse him of treason.

"If you let this man go, you are not Caesar's friend because whoever makes himself a king speaks against Caesar."

This frightened Pilate because he did not want to be accused of treason by the

Pharisees. So he brought Jesus out, then he sat down in the judgment chair.

With a gesture toward Jesus, Pilate said to the Jews, "Behold, your king."

They responded, "Crucify him."

"Do you want me to crucify your king?" Pilate inquired.

"We have no king but Caesar," the Jews cried out.

Pilate pronounced the sentence and sent Jesus to be crucified.

John reports that Pilate wrote a title and put it on the cross. The title was "Jesus of Nazareth, the King of the Jews." He wrote it in three languages so that many could read it. The chief priests demanded that he change the title to "He said he was the King of the Jews," rather than "King of the Jews."

Pilate refused to change. "It stays as I have written it," he said.

John reports that Jesus' final words were, "I thirst." After drinking the traditional vinegar of those crucified, he said, "It is finished" and died. His side was pierced with a spear just to make sure he was dead because it was a holiday time; the Sabbath was coming, and the body had to be taken down from the cross.

"I saw this, myself," reports John.

A Jew who was a secret follower of Jesus asked to take possession of the body. He and another secret follower anointed the body and wrapped it in the traditional way. They placed him in a nearby available burial place temporarily because of the holiday.

After the Crucifixion

John 20

Mary Magdalene went to sit by the burial place early the next morning and saw that the stone had been removed from the sepulcher. She ran to tell Peter and John that someone had moved the body and wondered if they knew where it had been placed.

John reports that he and Peter then went to the sepulcher and that he, John, got there first. Stooping down, he saw the linens the body had been wrapped in and the head covering wrapped together in another place. John went in, and then he believed that Jesus had vanished. He says they were not yet aware that the Messiah must rise again from the dead. Peter and John went home.

Mary stayed behind, weeping, and peered into the sepulcher (burial cave). John reports that Mary saw two angels sitting where the body had been and that they asked why she was crying. She told them it was because she did not know where the body was. Then she saw Jesus but did not know it was Jesus. She assumed he was the gardener and asked him to tell her where the body was. When Jesus said her name, Mary recognized him.

John reports that Jesus then said to Mary, "Don't touch me, because I have not yet ascended to my Father. But go tell my disciples I said, "I ascend to my Father and your Father, and to my God and your God."

She told them what she had seen and heard.

That same evening when the disciples were meeting secretly behind closed doors, Jesus came and stood among them and greeted them, "Peace be unto you."

Then he showed them his hands and feet. The disciples were very glad to see him. "As my Father sent me, even so I send you," he said. Then he breathed on them and said, "Receive you the Holy Spirit. You have power to forgive."

Thomas had not been at that meeting, so when the others went to him saying they had seen Jesus, he did not believe them. "I will believe it only if I can see and touch the print of the nails in his hands."

Eight days later, according to John, when the disciples were at their meeting place, Jesus appeared in the room again, even though the doors were closed, and said, "Peace be unto you." He invited Thomas to touch him so that Thomas could also believe that he had returned.

John reports that Jesus showed himself again to the disciples at the sea of Tiberius. Obviously Jesus did not have the same appearance that he had as a human form because in John 21:12, John says, "None of the disciples dared ask him, who are you, knowing that it was the Lord."

Then Jesus told Peter that it was now time for Peter to honor his commitment to the mission and that he would find himself needing to go into unpleasant situations.

Peter responded, "What is John supposed to do?"

John says that Jesus' response was that Peter should follow Christ as he understood his own guidance to be and to not be concerned with what John should be doing.

"What is that to thee? Follow me."

CHAPTER EIGHT

The Jesus Followers

After the crucifixion of Jesus, crowds of 50,000 people would gather in coliseums throughout the Roman Empire to watch followers of Jesus being slaughtered for sport. Because of this, the Jesus groups met secretly during the life and after the death of the apostles who had scattered far and wide to teach Jesus' message, according to their understanding.

During those early years of the apostles' work, one who hated the followers of Jesus the most was a militant Jew named Saul, perhaps named after the ancient King of the Israelites. He was a soldier and a bounty hunter who upheld the Jewish tradition and hated the troublemaker Jesus, who was already "dead" but whose influence was still very much alive. Saul, who later changed his name to Paul, thrived on tracking down followers of Jesus and bringing them in for the slaughter. Saul had heard about the apostles' report of seeing Jesus coming in a light body and of communicating with Jesus after his crucifixion. He believed they were using this story to make trouble among his people.

One day while Saul was crossing the hot desert in pursuit of Christians he was tracking down, an amazing thing happened to him. He said that he had become blinded from a brilliant light shining into his eyes and that while he was blind, a vision of Jesus came, speaking to him. Paul claimed that now he was going to be a leader of Jesus' followers. He reported that in the vision Jesus asked him, "Why are you persecuting my people?" (Remember, the belief of Saul and the Jews he represented was that a dead person sleeps, unconscious, in the grave until Judgment Day.)

Saul said that seeing a dead man still alive and not contained within the grave changed his mind. He had believed that Jesus was a liar, out to overthrow the Jewish religion and make fools of the Jewish people. Now he believed not only that Jesus was the Messiah, but that Jesus was actually God. This is what he began to teach. He gave up his position in the government, changed his name to Paul, and went to tell the apostles that he had been appointed by Jesus to teach people to accept Jesus.

The apostles were alarmed and questioned this. They had seen Jesus in the light and had experienced the presence of the Holy Spirit within themselves. Jesus had come several times to meet with them as a group, preparing them to teach and assigning each apostle a specific area within which to work.

Jesus had emphasized that he would keep nothing from them and that he considered them not as servants but as his friends and partners.

Because of this, they felt he would have informed them if he had assigned someone else to be a major teacher in the mission. Because he had not mentioned Paul and because Jesus had covered the entire geographical area in his assignments to them, they were skeptical of Paul's story. How could he deliver the message of the kingdom of heaven when he had not been trained as they had been, had been an instrument of killing those who had accepted the message, and had not understood the message of the kingdom?

They asked Paul what territory Jesus had assigned him to cover. He said that he had no limited territory but would be teaching wherever he wished to go.

Accepting him reluctantly, they recalled Jesus words to them from just before the crucifixion. Jesus had said privately to them that many would come in his name. He had told them, "You are my friends, not my servants. A friend knows what the master has in mind; a servant only does as he is told."

Territorial conflict arose.

Each of the apostles had been advised to teach according to his own understanding. But Paul's message, being quite different from that of the apostles, focused on the resurrection as proof that Jesus was God, on the requirement of reformation easy yoke that Jesus had promised.

Relentless in his efforts to gain followers and to control their meetings and their way of life, Paul would not cooperate with the apostles' efforts to have listeners hear a single message about Jesus.

 Eventually, the apostles let go of resisting his intrusion into their assigned territories and went about their business, some in hostility toward Paul, some ignoring him, and others co-operating with him. Even so, the Romans and the Jews were still turning them in and hunting them down for slaughter.

Jesus did not create a religion.

The word *Christians* was first applied by Jewish leaders and Romans to the followers of Jesus' influence. They were trying to stop the spread of Jesus message and used the term *Christian* as a contemptuous term to make fun of the believers. The Romans and the Jews believed that Jesus' followers were planning an uprising and continued to pursue and torture them. The Romans believed the followers wanted to take rulership over Jerusalem, the Jewish people, and the wealth of the religion.

The term saints, as used by some of the early followers of Jesus, was an identifying term carried over from the Essenes who called themselves the Brotherhood of Saints and who had been expecting and preparing for the teacher of righteousness. Other early followers merely called themselves Jesuits or Friends.

After accepting the name Christians for his followers, Paul used the terms Christians and saints interchangeably in his writings. Paul and his friends Mark and Luke did a great deal of writing. Paul's writings were in the form of letters to the spiritual groups he had set up as he traveled far and wide. Paul designed strict rules and regulations to govern the groups that he established, gradually forming an extension of the Jewish religion rather than a group of people breaking free from the old premises. He reprimanded his groups for openly questioning his teachings. He flagrantly dictated rules of conduct to his followers, something Jesus had never done.

Luke, a Greek scholar, attorney, and physician, collected stories of Jesus that would help Paul in his efforts. Paul had the belief that the Israelites and all of humanity were paying for the original sin of Adam and Eve. He taught that the only way to be forgiven by God was to admit that Jesus was God. He taught that humanity had but two responsibilities. One was to accept forgiveness for the original sin by pronouncing Jesus as God. The other was to cooperate with the rules of this new religion that he was forming.

Paul's desire was to establish a world-wide, powerful religion, and he taught that when this was accomplished, Jesus would come back and take his place as king of the world. The world would then be Eden restored.

People from non-Jewish backgrounds found his message very appealing. It helped them to define answers to some of their questions about life: Why do people have trouble? (It is God's punishment.) What do people need to do in order to prevent worldly troubles forever? (They need to make everyone accept Jesus as God.) What can we expect in the future after many have accepted him as God? (Eden will be restored on the earth, and Jesus will return as benevolent king of Earth eternally.)

Of course, this was the same as the Jewish philosophy had been, except that in Judaism one must try to please God without knowledge of how to do it and hope that someday forgiveness would come. Paul's message merely extended that philosophy to say, "But now you do know how to please God. Just say that Jesus is God and obey the rules that I am passing on to you from Jesus."

Jesus' efforts to have Jews reform their concept of God was lost in Paul's ministry.

Paul wrote many letters to his followers, as did the apostles. Because Paul traveled much more extensively and covered a wider territory than any other Christian teacher in his time, his concept of Jesus' message, identity, and mission was more widely known and accepted than that of the apostles who had traveled with Jesus and had studied directly under him.

Before the Books of the New Testament were Selected

In order to escape bounty-hunters, early Christians of different viewpoints (followers of the apostles, as compared to followers of those teachers who sprang up later) scattered to the shore of the Red Sea and the desert regions of Upper Egypt and to an island in the Nile River. They took their literature, art, and money with them and lived quietly in a monastic group style, or as hermits.

End of the Jewish World under Roman rule

In 70 A.D., about 10 years after the crucifixion of Jesus and during a Jewish rebellion against the Roman authority, the Roman Emperor's army responded by ransacking and literally destroyed many Jews and the city of Jerusalem, claiming possession of Jerusalem. However, they did not chase the Jews out of the city at this point. They were left alone to live there in poverty, among the rubble that had once been a fine city. (This happened in the lifetime of many who had heard Jesus predict the signs of the coming of the end of the world and that these signs would occur during their lifetime.)

Sixty years later, in 130 A.D., a new Roman Emperor began rebuilding the city of Jerusalem. Fearing that the Romans would move in to share the city with them the remaining Jews joined together to fight the Romans for possession of Jerusalem. After a three-year battle, the Romans literally cast the Jews out, scattered them in different directions, barred them from the city, and proclaimed it as a pagan city (a city that promoted the Roman's religious views).

The name of the city was changed to Aetia Capitolonia.

It was literally the end of the world for the Jewish way of life and the end of Jerusalem. They had considered their social system and the Holy City of Jerusalem to be their world, a world that God had given them in an ancient battle. Yet the end of their extended world, the Roman Empire, was yet to come.

In the third century after Jesus crucifixion, the Roman Empire was still strong and had become complacent with its power. The life for Christians was such that hermits who had gone to Egypt sealed themselves off from the rest of the world by living on top of pillars in the desert. Leaders of Christian groups were still inhabiting other parts of the Roman Empire, meeting in secret, but their hundreds of small manuscripts about Jesus' life and message were being circulated everywhere.

In the year 313 A.D., the Roman Emperor Constantine the Great, declared an end to the persecution of Christians in the Roman Empire. He said that he had experienced a vision of Jesus and was now himself a Christian. He sent out an order that Christians no longer needed to be in hiding. In fact, he pronounced Christianity as the required, official national religion of the Roman Empire and made a law that everyone must accept the Christian message. The name of the city of Aetia Capitolonia was changed back to Jerusalem, and it was given to all Jews who had turned Christian as a place to establish their Christian headquarters. Thus, we see that Jesus' foresight of how these social and political events would impact the Jews was quite accurate, and if Constantine did indeed see him, then Jesus, himself, had a voice in the matter.

A brief review of Jesus' foresight concerning the Israelites

- The end of the world for the Jews did come after much persecution and killing of the followers of Jesus before the fall of the Roman Empire.

- The Jews were cast out by the Romans into foreign and uncivilized regions (outer darkness) and were not able to act together as a group during the 1,000 years called the Dark Ages.

- The Jews who *had* accepted Jesus' message inherited the land that the

Jews had believed God gave to them.

- During those 1,000 years, the influence of the Christians grew strong and widespread, not because God did it, but because of the Roman's hatred for the Jews and because of the efforts of Jesus' followers.

- The fall of the Roman Empire, the end of that world reign and way of life, came about 100 years after Christian Jews were given the city of Jerusalem by the Roman Emperor and 100 years after the Roman Empire had accepted Christianity as its official religion.

In that year of their downfall, 410 A.D., when the fulfilled dreams of the Romans had produced an Eden of sorts for Romans and Christians, laziness and lack of purpose reigned. Citizens refused to join the military, and the territory was protected by only a few mercenaries.

Uncivilized barbarians built strong armies and used the element of surprise. They captured most of the Roman Empire, systematically and deliberately destroying the books and culture that the Romans had established. A time of ignorance and animalistic behaviors lasted for the rest of that millennium. Although the term millennium was not used, the concept of thousand-year astrological cycles had long been believed throughout the Mediterranean region as well as China. Due to astrology, the Jews and the Far East had been looking for a new star to emerge in the sky as a sign that the new millennium had begun, and that the messiah was born. With the fall of the Roman Empire, the arts and intellectual pursuits were all but forgotten by the majority of the people. Gluttony and overindulgence in every sense pleasure was the purpose for which they lived.

However, the Christians, whose core of worship by this point was life in small monastic groups, had hidden and preserved their ancient Jewish scriptures and the manuscripts written about Jesus. They also had stored Greek and Roman literature and art in their monasteries in order to preserve these things for future generations.

Before 500 A.D., Christians had spread the idea among themselves and had accepted a mission to reeducate and re-civilize the uncivilized people of the former Roman Empire. *They became the most powerful force for civilization in Europe.*

There were hundreds of thousands of Christians in this land which had been the massive Roman Empire but was now possessed and governed by barbarians.

These Christians were a mix of descendants of former Jews, and descendants of non-Jewish converts. Many of the Christian women lived in Abbeys which were group homes or group villages inhabited by nuns who opened their doors as retreats and learning centers to scholars. The Abbeys were centers for learning for both adults and children (the only schools available). The knowledge was available to any who wished to study in the learning centers, and there were many who accepted the invitation. The hunger for knowledge and beauty won.

- In 496 A.D. Clovis I, a barbarian leader of the Franks (France), was converted. He made Christianity the national religion of France.

- Soon afterwards the barbarian leader of Europe was converted to Christianity, and all the barbarians were required to accept Christianity.

- In that same century, Ireland was converted to Christianity by Saint Patrick.

- A hundred years later in the sixth century, Christian monasteries became accepted as sanctuaries and retreat areas for anyone who wanted to spend time in study and piety. They were thought of as centers for quiet culture, places of peace, reflection, and development of talents and development of knowledge in one's selected area of interest.

CHAPTER NINE
A Militant Form of Christianity Arises

At the same time this was happening during the fourth and fifth centuries, when this form of Christianity was being accepted by first one national leader and then another, a different concept of Christianity was developing strongly *in medieval Europe. It was based on Paul's model of staunch belief in the Jewish scriptures along with strict control by the leader and rules for the followers.*

While monastic Christians were working quietly to restore culture, art, literary knowledge, and individual pursuit of spiritual realization to the civilization, the

Paulian breed of Christians was developing toward a different goal. They wanted wealth and power.

Opposed to individual pursuits and individual interpretation, just as the Jewish religion had been, this group was focusing on a concept of one world religion enforced through fear of losing God's gift of forgiveness (Jesus) if one refused to join the church.

The threat was excommunication. Excommunication would be followed by hell for those who did not obey the dictates of the appointed religious leader. The appointed religious leader (pope) would be the final word in interpretation of religious rules. Kings would be subject to the *judgments of the pope.*

The administrative power of the papacy, ruling over moral questions of all people in one large land area in the European area of

Rome, was growing so strong that even their kings were afraid to question whether this was really Christianity. They consented to the authority of the pope and those who carried out the dictates of the pope. The bishop of the Roman Church was elevated above other bishops and chosen by a group of Roman Christian clergy as their pope. He was given, by this organized clergy, absolute power, and authority over all Christians and over the church.

The monastic groups, of course, were separate entities and not at all affected by or involved in this type of threatening and coercion. They were not accepted as members of the Christian Church or even as Christians by the pope who denounced them as heretics.

All letters and scripts of those early Christian teachers were preserved to some degree and passed down from era to era within their groups for quite some time.

A careful study of the letters of Paul compared to the other books of the New Testament will show many differences in opinion. The early Catholic religion was formed using Paul's concept of a worldwide religion, with Jesus returning someday to assume kingship over his people. Paul's rigid rules of conduct and continuation of the Jewish social structure were incorporated into that religion.

Hundreds of years after the death of all those earliest Christian teachers and writers, 27 books written by some of those early teachers were selected by a committee of Catholic leaders and bound together into a single book called the New Testament. This collection of small books was used as an addendum to the Jewish Old Testament, rather than standing by itself. This committee's choices were considered by the church as their final word on which of the many manuscripts about Jesus could be accepted as Christian scripture.

Thirteen of those 27 selected books were written by Paul. Three were written by Paul's followers. Two were written by blood brothers of Jesus, who had not believed him to be any more than an ordinary man until after the resurrection.

Of the remaining nine New Testament books, one was written by the disciple Matthew; two were written by the disciple Peter; five were written by the disciple John; and one (the book of Hebrews) was written by Apollos, a Greek scholar from Alexandria, Egypt. That is to say, the New Testament is a bound volume of books written predominantly by Paul and his followers. Christianity, as it was when those books were selected and bound together and presented as the sacred scriptures we see today, was clearly a religion founded by Paul and his followers and not by Jesus or his apostles.

For the first 100 years of this massive, organized, universal Christian religion, the title of bishop went often to the highest bidder. The Church frequently was divided by leaders rising up to offer different interpretations. These diverse leaders and their followers were called heretics by the pope, and they were excommunicated. Excommunication meant more than not being accepted as saved Christians. It meant that you would surely go to hell when you died. Many lived in fear of this belief.

The subsequent popes held to their goal of uniting all groups in Europe under the papal authority and continued to strongly denounce separate Christian groups. Each succeeding pope thought of himself as a spiritual heir of the Caesars of Rome, having been given the leadership of Rome by none other than Jesus. They even began to wear the imperial purple of the Caesars and to act just as the Pharisees had acted in ancient days.

The pope crowned princes, and if those princes misbehaved, they were excommunicated. The popes were the most influential men in medieval Europe. Imagining that excommunication meant a sentence to hell, even kings followed the pope's command.

At this same time, something called the Black Death ravished much of the world. Entire cities were destroyed by three fatal types of plagues. Because they did not know the cause of these plagues, they were perplexed when one person in a household would be spared, or one in a field of workers would fall, while the one next to him would remain healthy. They believed God was doing the killing and the selection because they did not realize that fleas and immune systems were the determining factors.

Many wars have been fought among Christians, with such a distortion of Jesus' message and mission that those who know the Master personally are sometimes reluctant to accept the title, Christian. But one who understands Jesus' message and recognizes what his mission was does not need to have a name in order to be his friend and an agent of his message of forgiveness, internal righteousness, and individual communion with God. The Holy Spirit, or Christ Spirit in each of us, is the One who will open the doors of our inner heaven and reveal its spiritual beauty, harmony, perfection, and goodness to us. In order to discover the divine presence with all its wisdom and love inside us, we need only to seek it, having faith that it is there.

ABOUT THE AUTHOR

As a child of three, Mary sat mesmerized on the backyard swing watching a bright light formed in the trees. As the light drew near, a face emerged in the light and spoke to her. The message was, "You are here to teach what you know of God".

Mary spent the first 40 years of her life learning and teaching while raising a family and seeing the world. Meditation, Prayer, An in-depth Study of World Religions and Practice of what came to her, occupied much of her spare time. After two NDEs and multiple visions of the Light, she finished her education and devoted the next 45 years to her ministry of direct spiritual teaching, spiritual counseling and writing. She is the founder of the Christian Mystics and Metaphysicians Society, A Path to Higher Consciousness and The Keys to Enlightenment Program. Mary is listed in multiple segments of Who's Who spanning from 2001 to 2022.

Other Books by Mary Saurer-Smith

A Comparison of World Religions

A unique examination of the history and life of the founders of each religion, this book explores differences and similarities of religions from ancient to modern day.

Windows of Life and Death

Spiritual autobiography of the founder of the Society of Christian Mystics and Metaphysicians, A Path to Higher Consciousness and The Keys to Enlightenment Program. Follow the author through her first Spiritual Vision at age three, two NDEs, a number of mystical experiences, and the revelations that followed.

The Master Teacher Within
A handbook describing seven techniques of meditation, step by step instruction, and the benefits of each.

Dynamics of Prayer
Explanation of how prayer works plus guidelines and exercises for developing an ongoing sense of the Divine presence.

REALITY The author's revelations and understanding of God's Divine plan and purpose. The soul's gradual evolution into complete Enlightenment and beyond is explained in easy-to-understand terms. Dark Night of the Soul, the Divine Plan, Spiritual Initiations are just some of the seemingly "mysterious" terms that are defined. This is a must read for understanding life, the potential for spiritual illumination and how to take charge of one's own development process of spiritual transformation.

Reincarnations of Rose A Quest of Many Lifetimes. Romantic, adventurous and intriguing short stories that trace the progressive lives of Rose. As she struggles with her desire to understand the truth about spiritual reality and how it relates to her purpose, we see Rose testing different views and coming into her personal realization.

Made in the USA
Coppell, TX
26 January 2024

28262725R00167